ROAD MAP TO HEAVEN

Road Map to Heaven

A Catholic Plan of Life

FR. ED BROOM, OMV

TAN Books
Charlotte, North Carolina

Cover design by DavidFerrisDesign.com

ISBN: 978-1-5051-1530-7

Published in the United States by
TAN Books
PO Box 410487
Charlotte, NC 28241
www.TANBooks.com

Printed in the United States of America

PRAISE FOR THIS BOOK

"Be a Saint." These words constantly echo in my heart through the many years of listening to Fr. Ed's powerful teachings, inspiring homilies, and spiritual guidance. Fr. Ed has planted in my heart the truth that we are made by God, for God, to be with God for all eternity. Road Map to Heaven is the perfect GPS for the most important journey in our lives. This little book was lovingly written, with God's grace, the power of the Holy Spirit, and the intercession of our Blessed Mother by a priest I consider a "living saint." A must-read for all!

> *Toffee Jeturian*
> *Couples for Christ USA National Director*

In this wonderful little book, Fr. Ed Broom maps out a plan to deepen your spiritual life in pursuit of heaven. Fr. Ed is an outstanding guide to direct us on the path to heaven with practical insights to help you strive for sainthood. Read the book, and then . . . follow the plan!

> *Cathy Fitzpatrick*
> *Associate Director of Adult & Child Faith Formation*
> *St. Martin de Porres Catholic Church*
> *Yorba Linda, CA*

CONTENTS

PART 1

INTRODUCTION

1

WHAT ON EARTH IS
THIS PLAN OF LIFE?

BEFORE outlining a methodical, organized, system-atic, cohesive, and practical plan of life, let us first try to explain this so-called plan of life. What on earth is a *plan of life?*

Order the Disordered

In the texts of the *Spiritual Exercises* of Saint Ignatius of Loyola, we read that one of the primary purposes of the *Spiritual Exercises* is to *order the disordered* in our life so that we can discover God's will and carry it out.

As a result of the sin of our first parents, Adam and Eve (Gn 3), disorder entered into the world on all levels: natural disorder, social disorder, family disorder, physical disorder, mental disorder, emotional disorder, moral disorder, and spiritual disorder—all of these became part and parcel of our very existence through sin. Mankind was adrift and the doors of heaven were closed to us until the coming of the Messiah. In his incarnation, life, passion, death, and resurrection, our Lord and Savior, Jesus Christ, came to restore order in the world and in our personal lives and, thus, to open the gates of heaven once more to God's most glorious creation, man.

Before we embark on any project, it helps to have a plan. For some projects, it is essential. This, the reordering of our lives so that they become more God-centered, is one such project that requires a plan. That is the purpose and the proposal for composing one's plan of life—to put in order the disorder in our lives. A well-composed and practical plan of life that is lived out can have incredible value in our lives and put us on the right path to arrive safely at and through the heavenly gates.

The huge majority of people do not know where they are headed, have no concrete purpose in life, and float around like so many leaves blown by the wind. They live with constant stress, anxiety, nervous tension, and very often suffer from depression, be it mild or severe.

On the contrary, the person who has a plan of life to live by has a huge advantage! He knows where he has come from—God! He knows where he is heading—heaven. He knows how to get there—Jesus is the Way, the Truth, and the Life. Finally, by composing and writing out a plan of life, he has given himself a spiritual road map so as to arrive at his final destiny—the kingdom of God! Therefore, we encourage you to compose and write out your own plan of life, your spiritual road map; in today's world, you may even call it your spiritual GPS! But no matter what you call it, its purpose will be to lead you to and keep you safely and securely on the highway to heaven.

It must be said from the start of this plan of life project that those who undertake this most noble enterprise of composing their personal plan of life must have the help of a spiritual director, some spiritual guide, some spiritual person to accompany them. Saint Ignatius of Loyola, as well as Saint Teresa of Avila, insisted on the dire need to have a director in one's spiritual life. The temptations, obstacles, and pitfalls in the spiritual life are far too numerous for anyone who seriously undertakes this spiritual journey to go along this way without some form of spiritual direction. Therefore, we warmly exhort all of those who plan to compose their own personal road map to heaven to secure some form of spiritual direction. We all have many blind-spots, and without the help of some qualified person outside our own experience, we can easily be deceived and tricked!

Forms of the Plan of Life

Chronological Plan of Life

There are several forms of the plan of life. However, in our short and humble work, we will be offering essentially two forms. You can do one or the other, or you can do both—the liberty of the sons and daughters of God! Each person should feel free to be open to the movement of the Holy Spirit in his or her life. Of course, this free movement should be moderated, guided, and checked by a trained spiritual director. God speaks through many channels, one of those being through the trustworthy guidance of a spiritual director.

The first form of the plan of life we would call or term a chronological plan of life. By chronological, we mean a plan of life in terms of a division in time brackets. This means that you want to step back and have an eagle's overview, an eagle's panoramic vision of the time that God has so generously given to you. Then, immersed in prayer, you want to humbly beg for the grace to make the very best use of the time that God has given to you. In other words, you do not want to be wasting time in this short life given to you by your Creator.

The time brackets can be divided into general and specific as defined in philosophical language. In each time bracket you want to discern and decide—with the help of the Holy Spirit and your spiritual director—what you would like to offer to the Lord. In other words, your plan of life is an offering, an oblation, a sacrifice that you want to give to God. If God has given you so much, should you not be ready and willing to give God something in return? Call to mind how much Jesus gave for you as he hung on the cross that first Good Friday, shedding every drop of his precious blood for the eternal salvation of your immortal soul. His love demands a response of love on your part. This is the spiritual motivation of the plan of life—to give yourself—your time, your efforts, your energy, your mind, heart, will, and whole being to God as an acceptable holocaust of love, thanksgiving, and praise!

Therefore, you want to look at the year and what you can offer to the Lord. Then scroll down to the month bracket and what your generous offering to the Lord can be. Following the month, of course, is the week. Much can be done in the course of the week. What are you willing to give to the Lord? Then move to the twenty-four hours in each day. A well-ordered and well-organized plan of life can offer to the Lord many golden nuggets in the course of these twenty-four hours! Now what about the hourly basis? Read and pray carefully over the text and see what you can give to the Lord during some hours in the course of the day. How about minutes and even seconds? In a word, God has given us all—we belong to God, and we want to give all that we have to our loving and almighty heavenly Father. We want to be generous with God. It is true that God cannot be outdone in generosity, but he is waiting patiently for our generous response.

Thus, we come to the conclusion of our chronological plan of life. It is a good practice to correct, modify, reform, and improve your plan of life at least on a yearly basis with the help of a good spiritual director.

Professional and Vocational Plan of Life

The second form of the plan of life is what we call the professional and vocational plan of life. We all have a universal vocation—to become saints! The plan of life can help us to pursue true sanctity of life. However, all of us have a particular and specific vocation in life. By vocation, we mean from the Latin *vocare*—calling! What might be specific vocations? Quick and to the point, the response would be the following: married, single, religious, priesthood. These are distinct and different vocations in life. The chapters included herein on the professional and vocational plan of life can best be applied to lay people engaged in the activities of the world. The faithful laity in the Church, the lay persons, are called to be the salt of the earth and the light of the world (Mt 5:13–16).

How then, you might ask, is this professional and vocational plan of life written out or organized? We have written several chapters on certain specific categories or areas in which you are invited to look at your life so as to analyze and examine with great sincerity and honesty how you are actually living out your call to holiness in each one. The first public preaching of Jesus was the following: "The time is fulfilled, and the kingdom of God is at hand; repent, and believe in the gospel" (Mk 1:15). The essential message is one word: *conversion*! The word transcribed from the Greek is *metanoia*, which basically means that we are all imperfect in many ways; we all have many disorders that come from original sin and personal sin, and we must change—leave the wrong, the disordered, the sinful, and put on the Lord Jesus Christ, the new man!

Therefore, specific chapters that we have outlined and explained are the following, with the earnest hope that you will sincerely look into these areas in your life and humbly admit that there is a real and urgent need to make some changes. Only God is perfect; the rest of us, each in our own way, are definitely *works in progress.*

Here is the list of specific categories or areas that will be addressed with regard to the professional and vocational plan of life:

- **Purity of Intention.** In your profession and vocation, learning *to do the ordinary with extraordinary love.*
- **Marriage.** 1) *As a spouse.* How can you improve and upgrade your relationship with your spouse, whom you are called to love until death do you part? 2) *As a father/ mother.* If God has given you the great gift of having children, how can you improve your relationship with your children? How can you bring them closer to God?
- **Work.** God calls us to work. God said to Adam: "In the sweat of your face you shall eat bread" (Gn 3:19). We are all called to work, but we can easily become lazy, negligent, cut corners, even fall into dishonesty. Part of the professional and vocational plan of life is to step back so as to view your work and see how you can make improvements. Never forget: the Lord is truly our Master. He will "pay us" according to our work; sometimes our labor will be less rewarded on earth, but that reward pales in comparison to what awaits the faithful servant of the Lord in heaven. What we sow is what we will reap!
- **Social Life/Network.** Maybe God is calling you to change a social or family relationship? Maybe God is asking you establish a new one? Be open to change!

- **Permanent Intellectual Formation**. As in all professions, how can you keep growing in the knowledge of your faith? What do you need to study to grow in your knowledge and love of God?
- **Apostolic Life**. If you love God, then you should love what God loves: the salvation of immortal souls! How can you be a better fisher of men?
- **Penitential Life**. Prayer and penance are the two wings on which you can fly high to God and to heaven! What penitential practices should you undertake? Jesus said, "Unless you repent you will all likewise perish!" (Lk 13:3).
- **Prayer Life**. What changes can you make in your prayer life to draw you closer to Jesus, draw you into deeper union with Jesus, your best friend?
- **Sacramental Life**. How is your reception of the sacraments? How can you be more fervent and faithful in your reception of the sacraments, especially confession and the most Holy Eucharist, the two celebrated most frequently and the "lynchpins" of the spiritual life?
- **Marian Element**. If we really do love Jesus, then we must love the one he loved most on earth, and that is his mother, the Blessed Virgin Mary. How can you establish a more filial and loving relationship with Mary who is our life, our sweetness, and our hope?

Hence, you are being called through prayer and spiritual direction, with utmost sincerity, to look into different categories in your professional and vocational life, to examine and analyze them, and to honestly admit that there is still much to be changed, not with sadness but with great gratitude! God is calling you to become a saint, and therefore, he is calling you into a deeper conversion of life. Beyond the shadow of a doubt, the writing out of this plan of life or road map to heaven, with the help of a good spiritual director, is one of the most efficacious tools to arrive at *ordering the disordered* in our unruly, confused, disoriented, and chaotic lives. This practice is highly recommended by Saint Ignatius of Loyola in the context of the *Spiritual Exercises*. If done well, you will never regret it; rather, you will be eternally grateful to God as you travel with speed and graceful ease on the highway to heaven!

2

WHAT ABOUT THE FOUNDATION OF YOUR HOUSE?

AT the very end of the Sermon on the Mount (Mt 7:24–27), Jesus presents us with a literary contrast that focuses on the foundation of a house. One house was built on rock; the other, built on sand. Both are houses.

Then it happens! A violent storm strikes both of these houses! Now we come to a keen awareness of the difference between the two houses which, from their outside appearance, seemed almost identical. Indeed, external appearances can be very deceiving. Man can see the exterior, but only God can read the inner depths and secrets of the heart.

Now the violent storm descends upon the house built on sand and the house rocks and rolls, turns and gyrates, and in a very short time, the house crumbles and collapses. Total disaster and ruin have visited this house built on sand. The reason for this disaster and total ruination of the house is clear and obvious! It had a very weak foundation— that of sand!

Once again, the violent storm descends. However, this time on the house that is built on rock, solid rock. Thunder, storm, rain, and wind batter violently against this house built on rock, for hours and even days. No problem whatsoever in the least! The reason? In contrast to the house built on sand, the rock foundation of this house can resist the most violent weather conditions in any time and place.

In a very clear and parallel sense, we can compare the two different house foundations to our own spiritual life, for the words and parables of Jesus have infinite value and offer us a timeless message, one accessible to all peoples everywhere, regardless of their culture. As we "unpack" this parable, consider the following:

- **Builder.** God is the builder who constructs every house. The Psalm reminds us: "Unless the Lord builds the house, those who build it labor in vain" (Ps 127:1).
- **The House.** The house is the human person, constructed by God himself.
- **Abandoned or Full House.** Once the house is built, it can be abandoned or it can be an invitation for inhabitants.
- **Foundation.** Those who build the house can choose a variety of foundation materials or structures.
- **Sand.** The choice of the foundation material can be that of sand.
- **Nature of Sand.** The obvious nature of sand is lack of solidity, lack of stability, lack of structure, lack of firmness; it can even be blown by the wind.
- **Metaphorical Sense.** In a metaphorical sense, sand can come and go, be present and absent, be seen and then disappear.

- **Rock/Brick/Cement**. On the other hand, there exist foundations of rock, brick, or cement.
- **Rock Foundation**. The essence or nature of rock is stability, strength, permanence, solidity, longevity.
- **God Is Our Rock**. The Psalmist actually compares God to a rock! God is strong, eternal, ever-lasting, faithful, now and always.

Having illustrated the stark contrast between the house built on sand and the house built on rock, let us apply this to our spiritual lives and the basic thrust of our work: *Plan of Life, to order the disordered!*

There is a story of a multimillionaire who bought an enormous plot of land on which to build expensive mansions with the purpose of selling them and making a huge amount of money. After gathering together all the elements needed to build these mansions—engineers, contractors, subcontractors, bricklayers, painters, plumbers, day laborers, and the various materials needed—the expensive mansions were built. Within a short period of time, the mansions were purchased. All the new homeowners rejoiced at their purchase. However, something unpredicted and unfortunate surprised them.

One of the owners began to complain upon noticing that his basement was caving in. Then another owner lamented over a bedroom sinking. Still another buyer angrily reproached the seller because the dining room floor tiles were separating. To make a long story short, the builder was unaware of the nature of the plot of land that he purchased, and these wealthy mansions were actually built over an old garbage dump. Consequently, all the houses had to be torn down and demolished, and the poor seller lost his profits, savings, and much more!

If our spiritual edifice is constructed on sand, then it will crumble and collapse. Our spiritual edifice must be constructed on solid rock, not sand! If we have chosen sand, then sooner or later, we will collapse, crumble, and disintegrate in our spiritual life!

The house built on mere sand is the individual who has little or no spiritual life. Or it might be somebody who has a spiritual life built on mere feelings and emotions. His feelings are his spiritual indicators. If he feels good, then he will pray to God. If not, he reasons, what is the purpose? This is the sandy foundation: the person who has little or no spiritual life or his spiritual life has a foundation based on mere whims. He is like a leaf detached from the tree falling, fluttering, driven by the wind. The wind determines its course. He is like the New England weather vane perched on the roof of the house that is blown in whatever direction the blows it.

The house built on rock is the individual who has God as his foundation. Feelings come and go, but they are not his master and mover. The man whose house is built on rock has his whole life—his thoughts, feelings, desires, motivations, and ultimate goal—directed towards God. This is manifested by having established for himself goals—long term, short term, as well as immediate. Motivation is the key word. He is motivated by a desire to get to heaven and to use all the practical steps to arrive at that goal.

What type of foundation do you have in your spiritual house? Is your spiritual life built on the sand of feelings, emotions, and the changing winds of fortune? Or is your spiritual life built on the Rock who is the eternal and everlasting God!

The goal of this work on the plan of life is to help all of us establish for ourselves concrete, clear, and practical objectives to carry out so as to arrive at our goal: the eternal salvation of our soul and union with God in heaven for all eternity. If God indeed is the center of our thoughts, desires, and decisions, then heaven will eventually be our eternal destiny. Jesus stated this very clearly: "What does it profit a man, to gain the whole world and forfeit his life?" (Mk 8:36).

The plan of life invites and challenges us to step back, peer into our lives with dead honesty, and ask ourselves the question: how are we using our time, our talents, and our treasures in relationship to God, eternity, and our ultimate goal which is heaven? We have to be transformed into the eagle soaring over the mountain, viewing in detail all that is below—the contour and colors of the trees, the rivers, the lakes, the ocean whitecaps, the animals large and small, the hills, the ravines, the stones, the leaves, all! In an analogous sense, this is how we must view our lives, our actions, and the direction in life that we are taking. Even though painful, we will come to a penetrating awareness that there are many areas in that huge landscape of our interior life that must be changed, cleared, uncluttered.

What is really being said here is that we must make an honest examination of conscience and admit that there is much to be changed, much to be converted in our spiritual life. Again, we look back to that first message in the public life of Jesus which should resonate in our ears always: "The time is fulfilled, and the kingdom of God is at hand; repent, and believe in the gospel" (Mk 1:15).

Composing a plan of life is a very concrete manner in which we can develop an honest and sincere working out of our conversion of life. Why not accept the challenge?

For this specific reason, as stated earlier, we offer you this humble work, this simple plan of life, as a remedy for your constant disorder. This plethora and wide variety of disorders fundamentally stem from sin and a lack of God in one's life. In other words, our God is a God of order; sin, on the contrary, wreaks havoc and causes universal disorder in our lives. The Holy Spirit is a God of order; sin disrupts this order.

Therefore, as we embark upon this wonderful journey from disorder to order, from sin to holiness, from the world to God, from sadness to happiness, let us lift up our eyes to the Blessed Virgin Mary. In 1531, Our Lady appeared four times to the humble Saint Juan Diego. The last appearance took place on Tepeyac hill on December 12, 1531, early in the morning. The sign that the bishop requested was growing on the cold and frozen hillside—a multicolored array of beautiful Castilian roses. Juan Diego scrambled to the place where the roses were growing, cut them, cast them into his tilma in a very disordered and unruly manner, and then brought them to the presence of Our Lady of Guadalupe. Before sending Juan Diego off to the bishop, Our Lady, with her own gentle hands—the hands that held Jesus as a baby and even his dead body—took and arranged the roses in a beautiful and well-ordered bouquet to present to the bishop.

Therefore, we would like to present this work to Mary, to Our Lady of Guadalupe, and beg her for this most special grace and gift: to *order the disordered* in our lives. We beg Our Lady to pray for us and to intercede for us before the throne of Almighty God, to help us become that eagle and see the panoramic view of our lives, to help us honestly admit the many disorders in our life—usually due to sin—and to help us to change, to be converted. How? Quite simply by reading carefully this humble work, written for the purpose of saving souls. But also that, through Mary's prayers, we will be able to hammer out a concrete, written plan of life, a road map to heaven, to *order the disordered*, and as a result, experience the peace that surpasses all understanding, the peace that only God can bestow upon us. Dear Mary, take our broken and disordered lives and order them with your gentle but firm hands so that we will be a sacrificial offering pleasing to Jesus the Lord.

3

A CHALLENGING BIBLICAL CHAPTER TO CHARGE US SPIRITUALLY

THE Gospel of Saint Matthew, chapter 25, can challenge us, get us charged up, and hopefully convert us
into utilizing our time, talents, and treasures in formulating
and living out a plan of life.

This chapter consists of three parables: the parable of
the wise and foolish virgins with their lamps, the parable
of the servants given talents from their master, and finally
the parable of the Last Judgment, where the sheep are separated from the goats by the Chief and Supreme Shepherd,
Jesus, who will come to judge the living and the dead.

In this brief chapter, we will focus on the parable of the
talents. The Master gives talents to his servants: to one servant, five talents; to another, two talents; and to the last servant, one talent. Then he goes on a trip. The Master expects
all of the servants to use, invest, and multiply the talents
that he has generously given to each one.

Upon returning from his journey, the Master meets with
his servants to render accounts—to see whether or not they
have used profitably the talents given to them. The first two
servants, utilizing most profitably the talents given, return

to the master double the amount. Upon receiving this good news, the Master compliments them and promises them even more. Indeed, they used their time, talents, and treasures well.

However, the condition of the last servant turns out to be quite different from the first two. Instead of investing the one talent and bringing forth a profit, out of fear, he buried it, causing it to be barren. Angry, the Master calls this servant a *wicked and lazy servant*! The talent that was given to him is taken away and given to the man who began with five but now has ten. As a punishment, the Master says with great severity, "For to everyone who has more will be given, and he will have abundance; but from him who has not, even what he has will be taken away. And cast the worthless servant into the outer darkness; there men will weep and gnash their teeth" (Mt 25:29–30).

What about us? How can this parable be applied to me and my plan of life? Quite simply! The Master is the Lord Jesus. He has given each of us time, treasure, and many talents. It is incumbent upon each and every one of us to humbly and gratefully recognize our most generous Benefactor, God himself, and all that he has so generously bestowed upon us out of the abundance of his heart. He has given us so much, truly so much!

An easy way to divide the riches that we have received from God is to step back and recognize the time he has given to us, the treasures he has so abundantly endowed us with, and the talents flowing from his infinite love and mercy. For the purpose of comparison with the parable of the talents, we will use the term *talents* as meaning all God's gratuitous gifts to us of time, talents, and treasures.

There is a modern slogan: *Use it or lose it!* This is the whole thrust of the parable of the talents. If we do not use these God-given talents, we can easily lose them. Cars left sitting on the street rust; muscles not exercised atrophy and turn flabby; musical talents not practiced degenerate into cacophony; cooking abilities not cultivated become a penance to the eaters, and health without constant supervision leads to sickness. So it is with our talents; if they are not used, they can be lost. In the parable of the talents, the Master is really Jesus who will come to judge the living and the dead, and he desires us to use to the very maximum all the talents that he has bestowed upon us.

A well-organized, methodical, and systematic plan of life will be of incredible value with regard to the proper use of our talents. Upon examining our lives in the light of God's goodness, generosity, and mercy, we come to a keen awareness that God has given us so much! This being the case, the Holy Spirit motivates us to recognize our talents and use them to the maximum, and not let them lie fallow and become useless. The plan of life is really a form of a practical prayer program. It is a recognition of the gifts received from the Giver of all good gifts and our response of love, returning the love of our generous and good God by using our talents well. In doing so, we become an *oblation* to

God; that is to say, an offering to God for all of his wonderful gifts.

One of our chief enemies in carrying out and living the Gospel parable of the talents is that of sloth, laziness—one of the capital or deadly sins. Our laziness can be of three kinds: physical (of the body), mental (of the mind), and spiritual (of the soul).

The remedy to not falling into the dangerous pitfall of the lazy man with the one talent buried in the ground is a well-organized, methodical, and systematic plan of life; one written and submitted to one's spiritual director for approval, so that the many temptations to be seduced into laziness can be surmounted. Then, instead of earning a sharp rebuke and chastisement, we will be well-regarded by the Master and receive not only a reward in this life but also a reward in heaven and eternal life!

We would humbly invoke the prayers and presence of the Blessed Virgin Mary to come to our aid. It was through the powerful intercession of Our Lady at the wedding feast of Cana that Jesus performed his first public miracle, transforming water into wine (Jn 2:1–12). So, we beg Our Lady to graciously ask Our Lord to transform our few talents into countless blessings!

PART 2

CHRONOLOGICAL DIVISION
OF YOUR PLAN OF LIFE

4

INTRODUCTION TO THE CHRONOLOGICAL APPROACH

W AYS in which this plan of life can be composed are without a doubt many! Experience in giving the Spiritual Exercises of Saint Ignatius of Loyola has proven that what is termed a *Chronological Plan of Life* is very efficacious.

Chronological

What do we mean by the word *chronological*? The word actually derives from Greek and refers to time. In other words, we will present your plan of life in brackets of time; that is to say, time divisions. Life is short; therefore, time is of the essence. We do not want to be wasting any of the time that God has so generously given us to save our souls and to work so as to save many other souls. Saint Alberto Hurtado, a Jesuit Chilean priest who died early in life of pancreatic cancer, stated with respect to time, "There are two places to rest: the cemetery and heaven." In other words, while we have our life's breath and ability, we should use our time to the maximum. On one occasion, Saint Peter Canisius, another saintly Jesuit and Doctor of the Church, was exhorted to slow down. His response: "I will have all eternity to rest; in the meantime, it is time to work for the salvation of souls."

Saint Augustine leaves us with a powerful image in these words: "Our life in comparison with eternity is a mere blink of the eye!" The Psalmist-poet expresses the same concept in these words, highlighting the ephemeral and transitory character of the human condition: "As for man, his days are like grass; he flourishes like a flower of the field; for the wind passes over it, and it is gone, and its place knows it no more" (Ps 103:15–16).

The first pope, Saint Peter, gives us this twist: "With the Lord one day is as a thousand years, and a thousand years as one day" (2 Pt 3:8). Before we know it, our lives will wind down and come to an end, and what will we have to present to God? Saint Paul reminds us: "Whatever a man sows, that he will also reap. For he who sows to his own flesh will from the flesh reap corruption; but he who sows to the Spirit will from the Spirit reap eternal life" (Gal 6:7–8).

The water that rushes impetuously under the bridge will never return again. So it is with time! When a year, a month, a day, an hour, a minute, or even a second has passed, it will never return again. Let us, through our plan of life, be misers for time so that we use the days, hours, and minutes of our lives to the maximum, for the sanctification of our own personal lives and the salvation of a rich harvest of souls for all eternity!

Why all this on time? For this simple reason! Composing

a clear, concrete, and practical plan of life will help us enormously so as not to waste time. By *ordering the disordered*, our tendency for wasting time will be greatly curtailed, and we will value time as one of the most precious gifts that God, in his great love and providence, has bestowed upon us!

Clearly Defined Blocks

Annually. Every year! Fine! Let us launch ourselves into the time-tunnel of our plan of life. Our proposal is, as the philosophers articulate it, to go from the general to the specific. That is to say, we will start with various proposals that can be done annually, on a yearly basis. Hopefully, at least once a year, we will look back on our plan of life and thank God for the many graces that he has bestowed on us due to our faithfulness to our plan of life, and then for the following year, add to it, so as to keep improving!

Monthly. From the yearly, we will move to the monthly time block. In the time block of a month, much can be accomplished with the help of God's grace. Unfortunately, much can be neglected or wasted. Our plan of life can keep us on the straight and narrow path.

Weekly. The month is divided into four weeks, usually with a few extra days. There is a huge difference between what a saint has done or will do in the course of a week and that of a person given to laziness. May this plan of life help us to imitate the saints! The Bible, from its start in the Book of Genesis, points out the fact that we should be working hard six days of the week and so merit our seventh day of rest. Our plan of life will help us to live out our weeks to the maximum!

Daily. Every day the Good Lord gives us twenty-four hours. Whether we live at the North Pole, Africa, or in the Sahara Desert, we all have twenty-four hours every day. We can divide our day into blocks of time: morning, afternoon, evening, and night—four different blocks of time composing one day. We are called to be like the eagle hovering over the mountain viewing with the utmost objectivity the dead wood, dried up leaves, debris, and trash that clutter the landscape of our life. The plan of life will help us to hone in and focus on, as if they were underneath a magnifying glass, the areas that have to be converted in our daily life. Let us join our hearts to the Psalmist: "This is the day which the LORD has made; let us rejoice and be glad in it" (Ps 118:24). Also: "Today, when you hear his voice, do not harden your hearts" (Heb 3:15).

Hourly. The hour can be divided into sixty minutes. It is interesting and helpful for our own personal examination of life to note how differently an hour can be used. For everybody on planet earth, an hour is sixty minutes. Mark this contrast! One person might use the hour to make what Venerable Archbishop Fulton J. Sheen calls the *Holy Hour* or *the Hour of Power*. That is to say, this Holy Hour is an hour of prayer spent with great reverence, respect, and love before Jesus present in the most Blessed Sacrament. Most profitable, don't you think? Another person could spend that hour plopped in front of the television viewing a soap opera where people use ugly words, dress immodestly, and for sixty minutes seem to compete as to who can break more of the Ten Commandments! What a stark and marked contrast! Hopefully, our plan of life will motivate us to really organize the hours of our life in the light of time related to eternity and the Judgment that we will all one day encounter. Jesus will come to judge the living and the dead.

Minutes. We have arrived at the minute; this, of course, is sixty seconds! A soul can be saved in that short span of time. That is to say, a death-bed sinner, even in the last minute or moments of his life, can open his heart and turn to God and be saved for all eternity. How easy it is to whittle away our lives, to waste the precious minutes that God has given to us. Never forget that the time we have is a gift given to us from the loving and providential hand of God! Our Lord reminds us: "He who is faithful in a very little is faithful also in much" (Lk 16:10). In a minute, we can easily pray the Our Father and even two Hail Marys—prayers very pleasing to God. Or perhaps we could make the powerful devotion of the Three Hail Marys every day of our lives part of our plan.

Seconds. Our plan of life accounts for even the smallest blocks of time that we call the *mere second*. We will leave as a surprise how even the small so-called second can be incorporated into our plan of life. Actually, nothing escapes the all-seeing eyes of God. As Saint Paul reminds us, quoting the Greek Poet, "In him we live and move and have our being" (Acts 17:28). May our time really belong totally to God now and for all eternity!

In the following chapters, we will present specific practices that we can undertake to fill in the gaps and use most profitably the time that God has given to us.

5

ANNUAL PLAN OF LIFE

Concrete Proposals for Every Year

THIS Psalm reminds us of the fleeting character of life, expressed in these words: "The years of our life are threescore and ten, or even by reason of strength fourscore" (Ps 90:10). Saint James, with his striking bluntness, reminds us: "For you are a mist that appears for a little time and then vanishes" (Jas 4:14).

Unsettling as it may be for many, nobody will live forever. Life in comparison to eternity is short; as Saint James attests, it is a mere puff of smoke. Saint Augustine coined this phrase: "Our life in comparison with eternity is a mere blink of an eye." In the open and close of an eyelid, our life terminates and Judgment immediately ensues.

Our Lady, who appeared six times in 1917 to three peasant shepherd children—Lucia, Francisco, and Jacinta—asserted, "If man would reflect on eternity, he would change his life immediately." Two of these little children, Jacinta and Francisco, would be taken within two years of the last apparition on October 13, 1917—Francisco at age ten, Jacinta at age nine. Lucia would live to age ninety-seven, dying on February 13, 2005.

The poet expresses the thought "time is of the essence!" Even the longest life—someone who lives into their hundreds—is still exceedingly short in comparison with eternity. If you like, eternity is forever and ever and ever, without end. May the Holy Spirit inspire us to be misers of time, to utilize our time to the very maximum! Then, after having faithfully carried out God's holy will in time, we can rest for all eternity in heaven. We were created for heaven, and all of our time, efforts, and energy should be exerted for one purpose: to win the prize, the eternal crown of happiness in heaven, with the Father, the Son, and the Holy Spirit forever!

What can we offer to god in the course of a year? We could decide to give in to sloth and do as little as possible; we are all endowed with free will, and God respects our freedom. However, this attitude manifests a lack of prudence, to say nothing of gratitude. Let us be generous with God as he is with us; the word that Saint Ignatius uses is that of *magnanimity*. This compound Greek word means "a great or generous soul." This should characterize our thought process, our decisions, our actions, our personality, our whole existence. God loves the generous and cannot be outdone in generosity. Saint Teresa of Calcutta said it with these words: "We should give until it hurts!"

This being said, let us get down to brass tacks and offer a series of concrete proposals that we can offer to God on a yearly or annual basis. Picture it in this light: these are gifts that we want to offer to God who has been so generous with us, giving us so much, even to the point of shedding his Precious Blood on the cross that Good Friday for the eternal salvation of our souls! If God has given us so much—really, so much—how much should we desire to give him in return? In other words, the love of God demands a loving response on our part.

An Eight Day Retreat. An excellent proposal, if at all possible, would be to get away to make a spiritual retreat. We all need to recharge our spiritual batteries every year. One of the best ways is by means of making a spiritual retreat; if possible, it might even be an Ignatian eight-day retreat. Every year for the past ten years, I have given an Ignatian eight-day retreat at the end of July, terminating near the memorial of Saint Ignatius of Loyola—July 31, the last day of July. As many as seventy-five people per year have participated in this retreat and the fruits have been indescribable! Of course, this requires organization and preplanning on your part. The decision cannot be made at a whim or overnight. Think about it, discern, and, if possible, act on this wonderful proposal.

Weekend Retreat. If it is not feasible for you to make an eight-day retreat, then possibly you could make a weekend Ignatian retreat, or weekend retreat in general! This does not require as much economically or as much preplanning. It is just a matter of looking into places, usually retreat centers, which offer weekend retreats.

General Confession. Saint Ignatius in the Spiritual Exercises strongly recommends that a *general confession* be made. When we say *general confession*, it does not mean generic, vague, or somewhat abstract. No! The *general confession* means to make a confession of the sins of your whole life, whether confessed before or not. Confessing sins already forgiven is called a devotional confession. We receive many graces from confessing sins already forgiven with more perfected contrition; that is, deeper sorrow for having hurt the One we love and who loves us. This helps purify our soul of the tendency to sin and removes some of the temporal punishment due to sins already forgiven. It means to sweep out the interior room of your soul of all of the dirt, to discard all the moral trash, to eliminate all the cobwebs, to burn all the dead wood and debris that possibly have been stored in the attic of your soul. It will take time and effort to prepare for your *general confession*, but it is definitely worth it! One of the many fruits that flow from a good *general confession* is deep peace of mind, heart, and soul that only Jesus the Divine Physician can give us. Indeed, Jesus came to heal and to save. This healing takes place most powerfully in the Church and through the sacrament of confession. As Jesus healed the many—the blind, the deaf, the paralytics, the mute, and even the lepers—he can heal your soul if you expose your moral wounds to him. Consult your confessor or spiritual director on how you might carry out this most noble enterprise of the *general confession*. You will never regret it! Saint Ignatius made

a *general confession* in the Marian Sanctuary of Montser-
rat, Spain, which took him four to five days. His life was
radically changed by this experience. Your *general confession* will not take four to five days, but the fruits will be
abundant, to say the least. Once you have made a *general
confession* of your whole life, it can be done yearly, renewing sorrow for and confessing sins of the past year, thereby
receiving many graces.

Reading the Bible: The Word of God. The Bible is the
Word of God. Saint Jerome, who was instrumental in
translating the Bible into Latin, after which it was translated into other languages, asserted poignantly, "Ignorance
of Sacred Scripture is ignorance of Christ." Indeed, we cannot establish a deep and loving friendship with Jesus if we
do not know who he is. In a year, with discipline and order,
this most noble enterprise of knowing Jesus through Scripture, starting with the four Gospels, can be accomplished.
The positive effects are innumerable. Use a simple but efficacious method to help you derive copious fruit. This is a
method you can utilize: 1) Pray to the Holy Spirit before
you read. 2) Pray the words of Samuel in the Temple:
"Speak, for your servant hears" (1 Sm 3:10). 3) Read Scripture prayerfully—it is God speaking to you; he wants to
communicate to you a message for the day. 4) Let the Word
of God touch your heart. 5) Speak to the Lord in your own
words. At the end of the year, your knowledge of Jesus, love
for Jesus, and friendship with Jesus will skyrocket, if indeed
you are open to his movements of grace.

Renew and Upgrade Your Plan of Life. There is a saying: If you do not row against the current, then the current will carry you downstream. The meaning? Either we progress in our spiritual life or we regress. The spiritual life by nature is dynamic. Growth in holiness and generosity is the goal! Changes can be drastic in the course of 365 days, one year. Hopefully, you will see such growth as the year draws to an end. Then as the year ends and the New Year is ushered in, you should want to give the Lord more in the new year than you did in the one that just ended. Highly to be recommended is that you pray to the Lord for a good spiritual director to help you discern what would be good to add to your plan of life, and what you would wish to add to it. Hopefully the Ignatian finality will become yours—to *order the disordered* in your life. May God help you!

6

MONTHLY PLAN OF LIFE

Be Holy as Your Heavenly Father Is Holy

LET us move now from the annual proposals to the monthly proposals. Every one of the twelve months in the year, God offers us countless opportunities to show our love for him through concrete proposals that translate into actions. Once again, we beg the Lord for the grace to *order the disordered* in our spiritual lives. The Holy Spirit is a God of order and discipline.

What then might be some proposals we can make and put into action monthly to show our gratitude and love for God, as well as our sincere desire to be holy as our heavenly Father is holy? All of these proposals in the plan of life have as their purpose to help us to live a more ordered, methodical, and disciplined life on our highway to heaven. How easy it is to veer off the straight, narrow, and demanding path that leads to eternal life!

As alluded to earlier in our conversations, we all must strive to find a competent spiritual director to accompany us on our arduous, demanding, and at times difficult path to our eternal destiny, heaven! In honest and sincere prayer

37

to the Holy Spirit, we should beg for the grace of discovering who would be the best spiritual director to connect us with God. Someone who can meet with us monthly.

As you are in the process of discerning through prayer who you might ask to be your spiritual director, you might be pondering, even questioning: What do I say to my spiritual director? A great question! On the top of the list, you should open up to your spiritual director about your *prayer life!* About my prayer life? Yes! You might approach your prayer life with the simplest questions relevant for a serious prayer life. Where should I pray? When should I pray? How long should I pray? What method of prayer should I adopt? What are some of the obstacles I'm encountering to growth in my prayer life?

What Books Should I Read About Prayer? Another essential aspect of your monthly spiritual direction meeting is to come up with a concrete proposal for reading up on prayer. In other words, you should discuss with your spiritual director what are the best book or books on prayer for you to be reading during the month. There are many books to choose from, and your spiritual director can help you discern the best one for you, given your time and interior life.

As mentioned in the annual proposals, a general confession of one's whole life is a real possibility. This being said, this should not replace frequent and well-prepared reception of the sacrament of confession, the sacrament of God's infinite mercy! The specific effect of the sacrament of confession is healing of our soul that we have wounded by personal sin. By means of analogy, what the doctor is to the body, so confession is to the soul. Confession serves as *healing* medicine, as well as *preventive* medicine. Actually, frequent medical checkups have as a purpose to prevent sickness. The same is true for frequent confession. An ounce of prevention, saves a pound of healing.

Prepare yourself well for your confession the night before. Give yourself a good block of time in silence with the Holy Spirit. Examine your conscience thoroughly with a good examination of conscience booklet. We are only required to confess mortal sins, the kind of mortal sin and the number. However, while we are not required to confess venial sins, it is a good idea to do so for the dual purpose of greater self-awareness and the building up of our resistance to committing even these smaller sins that wound and hurt us, others, and Jesus on the cross. Write down your sins on a piece of paper and take the paper with you into the confessional. Otherwise, you will find yourself remembering when you are halfway home something important that you forgot to confess! And remember to tear up the paper after confessing!

As a general rule, you meet your confessor in the confessional in the church. It is a good idea to have a regular confessor so that he can get to know you, know your strengths as well as your weaknesses, for then he is in a better position to help you, with God's grace, to conquer sin in your life and to *order the disordered* in your moral life.

The purpose of our plan of life is to establish order and discipline in a disordered life. Sin actually causes disorder; the Holy Spirit produces order and peace. Saint Augustine defines peace as *the tranquility of order*. Hence it is highly recommended to confess at least once a month! It is further recommended to establish a set day, time, and place to confess. Many choose to confess on the first Friday of the month to honor the most Sacred Heart of Jesus and as an act of reparation for their own sins and the sins of the whole world. *For the sake of His sorrowful passion, have mercy on us and on the whole world* (Divine Mercy Chaplet). Others choose to confess on the first Saturday of the month for the devotion of reparation to the Immaculate Heart of Mary, as requested by Our Lady of Fatima. The important thing is to choose a regular time to confess monthly and be faithful to it. (But, of course, if you unfortunately fall into mortal sin, you should not wait for your monthly confession but go as soon as possible.) As for a place to confess, preferably at the same place with the same confessor, in order to enhance your spiritual growth and spiritual benefits as noted above. Planning and being faithful to frequent confession, at least every month, is a very important proposal to advance in the spiritual life! Indeed, if we are looking for peace of mind, heart, and soul, undoubtedly frequent confession is a must, as confirmed in the lives of the saints—many of whom went even weekly to this great sacrament.

Changing the focus a bit, let us move from the purification of our soul through confession to further purifying

our soul by living out the gospel of charity in the service of others. When all is said and done, our judgment before Our Lord and Savior Jesus Christ will be based on obedience to his commandments: "If you love me, you will keep my commandments" (Jn 14:15). But our judgment will also be based on whether or not we have lived out the greatest of all commandments—love of God and love of neighbor! Jesus stated starkly: "Not every one who says to me, 'Lord, Lord,' will enter the kingdom of heaven, but he who does the will of my Father who is in heaven" (Mt 7:21). Therefore, let us love God in our neighbor, not only in word, but also in deed!

To put flesh and sinews on your plan of life, we invite you to read the Gospel of Saint Matthew, chapter 25. In the last section of this most challenging chapter, referring to love in action, Jesus mentions what the Church has named *the corporal works of mercy*. They are the following: feed the hungry, give drink to the thirsty, clothe the naked, welcome the foreigner, visit the sick, and visit those in prison.

Now through prayer and spiritual discernment, with the help of your spiritual director, decide on at least one corporal work of mercy that you believe God is inspiring you to carry out monthly, and then do it! Never forget that by carrying out this act of mercy, it is really Jesus whom you are serving in this needy person. His words are unequivocal on this point: "Truly, I say to you, as you did it to one of the least of these my brethren, you did it to me" (Mt 25:40). Get ready for your final exam by living out the gospel of love!

Saint John of the Cross expresses this truth poetically: "In the twilight of our existence, we will be judged on love." May your plan of life motivate you to live out *active charity* so as to prepare an everlasting home in heaven for yourself and those you serve!

7

WEEKLY PLAN OF LIFE

Six Days to Work and a Seventh to Rest

THE first book of the Bible, the Book of Genesis, states that God's work of creation took six days and then on the seventh day, God rested. Sunday, known also as the Lord's Day, is the day of rest.

Therefore, we must enter into the full context and meaning of the other six days of the week, leading up to Sunday, the Lord's Day! These days are designed by God for our own welfare and benefit, a benefit that comes to us through hard work.

After Adam and Eve committed the Original Sin, God chastised Eve and all women with the suffering entailed in childbirth. All mothers keenly know the pains of a pregnancy, the suffering in giving birth, as well as in raising children in the fear of the Lord. Likewise, man was given a chastisement, a suffering as a result of Original Sin. Different than the woman, man was called to labor, to work hard, and earn his bread with the sweat of his brow (Gn 3).

Despite the suffering involved, work, which is part of our plan of life, bestows many blessings. These are a few:

43

- When we work, we collaborate with God in perfecting the earth.
- Work helps us to develop the talents that God has given to us.
- Work, well done, serves as a means to help others.
- Nor should we neglect to mention the very true reality that idleness is the workshop of the devil; consequently, work actually diminishes many of the fiery darts that the devil launches at us.

Therefore, let us delve into the dynamic of our week and discern what we can offer to the Lord as the first fruit of gratitude for all that he has given to us. In a real sense, all the good we have is a sheer gift from God, and we crown God's creation when we use these gifts properly and generously.

Getting Started with Weekly Proposals for Sundays and Fridays

In a week's time, God created the world. In a week's time, collaborating generously with God, we can offer the Lord copious fruits for our own benefit and that of our brothers and sisters. Here we go!

Sunday: a day of rest! It should be obvious to all the followers of Jesus that Sunday is the Lord's Day, the day of rest, and should be for us the most important day of the week. It is not like all the other days of the week. Rather, it is a special day on which the Lord rested, and he wants us to rest on that day too!

Sanctify Sunday by holy Mass. It is a sad fact that most Catholics do not attend Holy Mass on Sunday; this must change! Sunday and the Holy Sacrifice of the Mass is the heart, core, and center of our weekly worship. In your weekly plan of life enthrone at its center the Holy Sacrifice of the Mass. God comes down from heaven in the Consecration so that he might be united to us in Holy Communion and fill us with his love, joy, and holiness. Maybe step it up by inviting some lost sheep back to Jesus, the Good Shepherd, who anxiously awaits us with Word and Sacrament in the Holy Mass, in the Holy Eucharist, in Holy Communion.

Friday, the weekly day of penance. Jesus stated unequivocally in the Gospel: "Unless you repent you will all likewise perish" (Lk 13:3). None of us should play Russian roulette with the salvation of our soul! This is a divine mandate. That is to say, Jesus commands it; therefore, we should humbly submit to dis holy will. The practice of weekly penance—specifically on Friday, because it was the day that Jesus suffered and died for us on the cross—is an ecclesiastical mandate. In the past, Catholics were required to abstain from meat on Fridays. Now we may choose some suitable form of self-denial and mortification in prayerful remembrance of the passion and death of Jesus.

The penitential actions are limitless, but we can mention a few to fill in your weekly plan of life. As a rule, better to choose a few that you will be faithful to than to have a multitude of proposals that go up in smoke. These concrete actions will serve to strengthen your willpower and once again help you to *order the disordered.*

Some Suggestions for Weekly Penances

- You might simply try to eat less on Fridays. Or, as some do, choose to not eat meat on Fridays.
- You might deprive yourself of a meal.
- Instead of drinking what you like, drink water.
- You might renounce all condiments. What? No salt, pepper, mayo, salad dressing, cream and sugar in your coffee, or sugar on your cereal, etc.
- Who knows, maybe there is some TV program that you really like to watch, and the Holy Spirit is challenging you to fast from viewing it!
- Possibly you have an addiction to your mobile phone, tablet, iPad, laptop, in the sense that you go overboard. Why not at least limit its use. This can be a good fast for the Lord!

The next two proposals may begin as weekly proposals on Friday, in view of all that Jesus willingly suffered for your salvation, but they will be most pleasing to the Lord if they become daily proposals! The reason for this will become evident as you pray on these very important penitential acts!

- A great fast would be that of learning to control your tongue. In other words, during the course of the day, avoid gossip, lies, detraction—using the tongue as a means of destroying others; even if what you say is true, you have no right to say it. (Read James chapter 3 on *Sins of the Tongue.*)

- You probably remember that as holy as he was, King David plunged into the depths of sin—adultery with Bathsheba, then killing her husband, an innocent man and one of his loyal soldiers, Uriah, the Hittite. However, as a prelude, these sins were preceded by David not controlling his eyes! He gave in to lust of the eyes before he gave in to lust of the flesh! There is a saying: *The eyes are the mirror of the soul.* Jesus leaves us this powerful verse from the Beatitudes: "Blessed are the pure in heart, for they shall see God" (Mt 5:8). Therefore, another proposal that can be carried out is the fasting of the eyes. This means trying to make a concerted effort during the course of the day to look only at things that are pleasing to God—the true, the noble, and the beautiful!

Of course, part of our plan of life related to our weekly proposals should be first and foremost, attendance at Holy Mass on Sunday, and if we are well disposed, the worthy reception of Jesus in the Eucharist.

More Weekly Proposals—Our Apostolic Life in the Parish

Our prayer life should spontaneously flow into our active life. In other words, a true contemplative life—that is to say, a life of deep prayer—should produce abundant apostolic fruits. True contemplation leads to fervent action! Jesus pointed this out with utmost clarity in the image he gave us of the vine and the branches (Jn 15:1–8). Jesus says that his Father will cut and cast into the fire the branches that do not produce fruit, but the branches that do produce fruit, he will prune. Why? So that we can produce more fruit, and fruit in abundance!

This important point must be expressed clearly: without a deep prayer life that leads to deep union with Jesus, the apostolic fruit we yield will be very limited. For that reason, Venerable Archbishop Fulton J. Sheen states: "First Come, Then Go!" Jesus is the vine; we are the branches. We must first cultivate deep union with Jesus through a deep contemplative prayer life, then we can give abundantly. We cannot give what we do not have!

If we truly love the Lord Jesus Christ, then we should indeed love what he loves. At the top of the list of priorities in the Sacred Heart of Jesus is his love for the eternal salvation of immortal souls. The Angelic Doctor, Saint Thomas Aquinas, asserts that one immortal soul is worth more than the whole created universe! The proof? The Precious Blood that Jesus shed for all of humanity and for each of us individually on Calvary that first Good Friday.

This being the case, we should all have a burning fire within our hearts—the fire that burned in the most Sacred Heart of Jesus—to collaborate with him in the salvation of immortal souls. Call to mind the words of the Lord Jesus:

"What does it profit a man, to gain the whole world and forfeit his life? For what can a man give in return for his life?" (Mk 8:36–37). And, "I came to cast fire upon the earth; and would that it were already kindled!" (Lk 12:49).

Therefore, let us offer a list of apostolic initiatives that we can carry out on a weekly basis so as to work side by side with the King, the Lord Jesus Christ, in the most noble endeavor of the salvation of immortal souls.

Saint James offers us these encouraging words with respect to bringing souls to God and our own salvation: "My brethren, if any one among you wanders from the truth and some one brings him back, let him know that whoever brings back a sinner from the error of his way will save his soul from death and will cover a multitude of sins" (Jas 5:19–20).

Consider, then, the following list of possible weekly apostolic initiatives that you might consider adding to your plan of life. Bring these initiatives to your spiritual director so as to confirm what is truly the will of God for you. We cannot emphasize too much the importance of seeking out and relying upon adequate spiritual direction so as to discern God's will and implement concrete actions in your life. God often speaks through the human channel of a spiritual director.

- **Catechism Class for the Children**. Jesus said: "Let the children come to me, do not hinder them; for to such belongs the kingdom of God" (Mk 10:14). Therefore, if you have a well-grounded formation, approval of the pastor and his encouragement, why not dedicate a time each week to teaching the little ones about knowing and loving Jesus the Lord, who loves them so much, and their purpose in life: *To know God, love God, and serve God in this life, so as to be happy with him forever in heaven.*

- **Confirmation Class for the Teens.** One of the groups most attacked by our post-modern, sensual, hedonistic, and even atheistic society is the teens. This being the case, it is imperative that parishes launch well prepared Confirmation programs to save our young people from plunging into a pit of sensuality leading to sin, then slavery to sin. If you feel you have the gift, the qualifications, and the preparation to serve in this area, offer your services to your pastor and parish so as to teach the young people, the teens, the true and ultimate meaning of happiness: knowledge of God who created them out of love, love for Jesus who suffered so much for love of them, and fear of the Lord—fear of offending him and a desire to obey his commandments.

- **Mentoring Program for Couples Preparing for Marriage.** An important program implemented in the parish of St. Peter Chanel in Hawaiian Gardens, California, is that of the mentoring program for couples preparing for marriage. This consists of having a married couple, who has been married usually for at least ten years, meet with an engaged couple preparing to get married, so as to mentor them. How? Praying with them, teaching them, catechizing them, and giving them practical advice to help them live out to the fullest the sacrament of Holy Matrimony—and this once a week over a period of several months. Maybe God is calling you to give an hour each week to this most noble initiative.

- **Visiting the Sick in the Parish and Encouraging Them.** Maybe you feel called to love Jesus who is truly incarnate in the sick of every age—children, teens, adults, seniors. Why not write down in your plan of life to give an hour of your time visiting a sick person, whether in the hospital or at home, who so ardently desires the company, the presence, the joy and engaging smile of someone, like yourself, and in this way bring Christ to them. Never forget the words of Jesus: "As you did it to one of the least of these my brethren, you did it to me" (Mt 25:40).

- **Bringing the Eucharist to the Sick.** After Mary gave her consent to God through the Archangel Gabriel—"Behold, I am the handmaid of the Lord; let it be done to me according to your word" (Lk 1:38), "And the Word became flesh and dwelt among us" (Jn 1:14)—then Mary went in haste to visit Saint Elizabeth, to bring Jesus to her cousin in her need. You may feel called to do the same: to bring Jesus to the sick—who are longing for a visit from him—but through your hands. Why not look into this?

- **Bible Study Group**. The Church strongly encourages us to read, meditate on, and get to know the infinite riches of the Word of God. So much so that the great Bible scholar Saint Jerome stated, "Ignorance of Sacred Scripture is ignorance of Christ." With permission of your pastor, maybe you can start a Bible study group in your parish or participate in one that already exists. Fill yourself with the Word of God so that you can give it to others, in imitation of the Blessed Virgin Mary.
- **Welcoming Others**. Who knows if once a week on Sunday, the day of the Lord, you may decide to become part of a welcoming ministry? This is a very simple apostolate, but at the same time, a very important one! It consists of welcoming people at the entrance of the church. The key to the success of this ministry is your smile. First smile, then greet and open the door! How many people have been turned off to the Church because of a cold reception? How many have been brought back when met with a radiant and welcoming smile! You do not have to limit your welcome to the doors of the church either; continue that welcoming spirit to all you meet. Invite newcomers to the parish to your home to share a meal.
- **Walk the Streets and Knock on Doors**. Once again with the permission of your pastor, maybe you feel called to go after the many lost sheep in your parish by walking the streets and knocking on doors once a week. Many of the wandering and lost sheep of the flock may

return if we take the initiative to seek them out! Why not form a team? How does this work in practice? You knock on the door of each house and ask if any Catholics live there. If they say *no,* you thank them and move on. If they say *yes,* you ask to speak with them, and you tell them you have brought gifts for them. Be sure to have with you many rosaries and parish bulletins listing the times of the Masses, confessions, and other parish services to give out to these lost sheep. If you like, holy cards of Divine Mercy and of Mary are always well received! Be prepared to listen to their questions, their concerns, and their sufferings. Be prepared to pray with them. Many lost souls are like ripe fruit ready for the picking! Go out ready to reap the harvest! Many lost souls are like fish in the water, lacking only the dropping of the nets. Why not drop the nets for an abundant catch of souls? We are all called to be *fishers of men!*

- **Sing to Your Heart's Content**. Maybe you are endowed with musical gifts? Saint Augustine encourages us with these words: *He who sings, prays twice.* Why not give an hour of practice each week with one of the choirs in your parish and then offer your heart, mind, and voice in song to live out the Sunday day of praise and worship with a harmonious melody flowing from the depths of your soul?

- **Any Parish Group: Get Involved!** *Do not ask what your parish can do for you; rather, ask what you can do for your parish!* Get involved! Do not sit on the sidelines or be a spiritual *benchwarmer*—that is, a passive observer. For the love of God and your neighbor, get involved in one way or another. Take a step back and observe what are the various groups and activities in the parish, then decide to become an active member in one of them! Or with the permission of your pastor, start a new one! We, who have received so much from the bounteous love of the Lord Jesus, are all called to give!

The Church and the parish is indeed a family. All members of the family must not only receive, but learn to give, and to give with magnanimity—meaning with great generosity of heart! May the Lord Jesus be our shining example! Not only did he give, but he gave every drop of his Precious Blood on the cross for our salvation. What are you ready to give in your weekly plan of life to show your love for him?

Still More Weekly Proposals — The Lenten Model/The Least of These

In the first set of weekly proposals, we highlighted the importance of keeping the Lord's Day as a day of rest, but even more important, keeping the Lord's Day Holy by attending Mass on Sunday and participating fully, actively, and consciously; and the importance of penitential acts which Jesus himself said are necessary for our salvation, offered specifically on Fridays, the day Jesus suffered and died for us on the cross. We offered a list of possible penitential practices to this purpose.

In the second set of weekly proposals, we highlighted the importance of *First Come, Then Go*—the maxim of Venerable Archbishop Fulton J. Sheen. Meaning first we come to Jesus, then we go to others. We do this by first cultivating a deep and contemplative prayer life that leads to deep union with Jesus. Then, loving what Jesus loves most—the salvation of immortal souls—we are ready to work side by side with him in this most noble enterprise of saving souls! To this purpose, we offered a list of apostolic endeavors centered in the life of the parish family.

In this third set of weekly proposals, we are offering the Lenten Model for your enlightenment, edification, and encouragement to help you return to our good God what he has bountifully given to you!

Let us recall the proposals on Ash Wednesday. The Gospel reading for Ash Wednesday presents three practices that can serve as a model and stimulus for living your plan of life, three practices to live out a pathway to holiness. These practices, found in the Sermon on the Mount, are the following: prayer, fasting, and almsgiving.

Now look over your week and the time that God has so generously given to you as a gift and see what you can offer to the Lord in return, focusing on these three classical practices of prayer, penance, and almsgiving. Sometimes the greatest penance is sacrificing your time!

- **Praying the Stations of the Cross**. This is a wonderful practice, highly recommended by the saints, in which you move from one station to the next contemplating the passion and death of Jesus. There are fourteen scenes in which you follow our loving Savior, Jesus the Lord. As you contemplate each scene, be present there with Jesus, then offer a prayer of thanksgiving to the Lord who suffered so much for your salvation. This practice is recommended highly, not only on Fridays during Lent, but on every Friday throughout the year.

- **Almsgiving.** Moving from seeing the suffering Jesus in the Stations of the Cross, now look for the "suffering Jesus" in our world today. The practice of almsgiving, interpreted in a more global sense, can refer to any act of charity that you offer to any person in need. Recall the words of our loving Savior: "As you did it to one of the least of these my brethren, you did it to me" (Mt 25:40). Beg the Lord to help you to see how you can live out the Gospel of charity and practice almsgiving to your neighbor.

- **The Most Vulnerable in Society.** Jesus said, "I came that they may have life, and have it abundantly" (Jn 10:10). The worldwide promotion of abortion, euthanasia, and physician-assisted suicide presents grave threats to the lives of babies in the womb and the elderly, making them among the most vulnerable in society. In his encyclical *Evangelium Vitae* (*The Gospel of Life*), Pope Saint John Paul II defended the sanctity of human life: "Man is called to a fullness of life which far exceeds the dimensions of his earthly existence, because it consists in sharing the very life of God. The loftiness of this supernatural vocation reveals the great-ness and the inestimable value of human life even in its temporal phase" (*Evangelium Vitae*, 2). This great pope and saint for modern times condemned this growing and widespread *culture of death* (*Evangelium Vitae*, 12). He gravely acknowledged: "All this is causing a pro-found change in the way in which life and relationships between people are considered. The fact that legislation in many countries, perhaps even departing from basic principles of their Constitutions, has determined not to punish these practices against life, and even to make them altogether legal, is both a disturbing symptom and a significant cause of grave moral decline. Choices once unanimously considered criminal and rejected by the common moral sense are gradually becoming socially acceptable" (*Evangelium Vitae*, 4).

• **Protect the Unborn.** Given the vulnerability of the unborn, you might prayerfully consider and discern with the help of your spiritual director if you are called to become active in pro-life ministry as part of your plan of life. There are numerous ways to witness to life and promote life in this ministry on a weekly basis: praying in front of an abortion clinic, sidewalk coun-seling for women entering these clinics, hotline coun-seling for women in crisis pregnancies, volunteering at or financially supporting pro-life clinics. The list is end-less! *Priests for Life and their national director Father*

Frank Pavone offer support and information, and coordinate pro-life activism: www.priestsforlife.org

- **Visit the Elderly.** There is a strong tendency in our society to give more importance to the young, beautiful, wealthy, witty, and intelligent to the detriment of the elderly, all too many of whom are neglected, forgotten, cast aside. Pope Francis terms this the *Throwaway Culture.* In other words, the sick and elderly are often seen as a burden to society, not worthy of attention. This thinking is part of the *Culture of Death* identified and condemned by Pope Saint John Paul II. It is important for us to promote a *Culture of Life*, not only for the unborn, but for the elderly as well! Therefore, a very important addition to your plan of life might be to give time and attention to visiting the elderly in their homes. You might propose this on a weekly basis.
- **Nursing Homes.** As an alternative, why not set aside time once a week to visit the elderly in a nursing home? Why not visit someone who is truly poor, lonely, abandoned, rejected, and forgotten! It is all too true that some of these elderly people never have visitors! And they may live like that for ten years before they die. Do this for the love of Jesus. Try to see Jesus in this person; see that he or she really is the poor and suffering Jesus.
- **Bring a Group.** Go beyond a mere visitation to the nursing home. Go with a group of "missionaries of love." What can you do? Together you can smile at and greet many lonely elderly persons. Pray with them. Sing

songs to them. Listen attentively to them, even if they repeat themselves constantly. Bring them a holy card and rosary and pray the Rosary with them. If they are unable to pray the Rosary, let them hear your group praying the Rosary for their intentions! The more abandoned, sick, lonely, and neglected the individuals, the more pleasing is your service to Jesus!

Final Weekly Proposals — Now in the Family!

One of the modern expressions or definitions of the family is *The Domestic Church* (Documents of Vatican II). Pope Saint John Paul II stated that the family is the basic building block of society. He also stated, "As the family goes, so goes the nation, and so goes the whole world in which we live" (Homily in Perth, Australia, 30 Nov. 1986). In other words, when the family comes unraveled, the society falls apart as well! This has been proven in the history of civilization!

Therefore, let us offer a weekly plan of life that we can aim at implementing with respect to living out our family life for the greater glory of God. Our desire and purpose is to form holy, happy, and wholesome families. Families are being rent asunder, and we must utilize all the tools that God gives us to form good families, to strengthen families, and to protect families from the onslaught of evil that engulfs and submerges many families, resulting in the children being mortally wounded.

Therefore, let us plunge into our family weekly plan of life and offer this to God as a generous gift for our good, the good of the whole society, and the good of the world at large!

- **Family Rosary**. Families should set aside time to pray together. Call to mind the immortal words of the Rosary priest, Venerable Father Patrick Peyton: "The family that prays together, stays together." With respect to the world, Father Peyton commented, "A world at prayer, is a world at peace." Starting now, why not decide to find a day, a time, and a place to pray the family Rosary. Ideally dad, the father of the family, will take the initiative to lead the family Rosary, but we don't inhabit an ideal world, so if dad is not a man of faith or is not in the house, mom can lead or even the eldest child. You can have family members take turns. This habit of praying the family Rosary will prove to be an infinite source of grace for the family, a sign of growing in grace, and a signpost on the highway to heaven.

- **Weekly Family Outing: Fun Time!** Given that we live in a fast-paced society, where we seem to never, so to speak, *have time*, families must stop this rat-race pace and find at least one day a week to be together as a family to rest, relax, and enjoy each other's presence! Also, whatever the activity may be, let it be done without the interruption of the cell phone!

- **Sunday Picnic!** As a follow up to the preceding idea, why not set aside time for a family picnic, possibly on Sunday after Holy Mass and Holy Communion. You have received Jesus in your heart; now encounter Jesus in your family; encounter Jesus in your loved ones! Maybe go to a park to play sports or on the playground!

- **Nature Walk**. A nature walk makes a great family activity. Find a trail, hill, seashore, or lakeside—some beautiful scene where you can walk, talk, and enjoy the beauty of God's nature along with your loved ones. God indeed is present in all times, places, and circumstances, in nature as well as in people. Open your eyes to contemplate the greatness and beauty of God that surrounds you. As Saint Paul recalls, "In him we live and move and have our being" (Acts 17:28).

- **Movie Time**. Why not find some day or night of the week—maybe Saturday or Sunday—to view a good movie together. Two classic family movies are *The Greatest Miracle* (2011) and *Miracle of Marcelino* (1955). (We can only recommend this older, authentic version.) Over the past twenty years, many good DVDs have been produced, especially on the lives of the saints. Their lives are fascinating and inspiring! Here are some to view and enjoy: Sts. Francisco and Jacinta Marto (*The Miracle of Our Lady of Fatima*, 1952), St. Bernadette (*The Song of Bernadette*, 1943), St. Maria Goretti (*Maria Goretti*, 2003), St. Jose Sanchez del Rio (*For Greater Glory*, 2012), St. Josephine Bakhita (slave to saint), St. Giuseppe Moscati (Doctor to the poor), St. Mother Teresa, St. Faustina, St. Therese, St. Padre Pio, St. Damien of Molokai, St. Francis of Assisi, St. Anthony of Padua, St. John Bosco, St. Philip Neri, St.

Ignatius of Loyola, St. Teresa of Avila, St. John Vianney Cure of Ars, St. Rita of Cascia, St. Augustine, and
the popes—Venerable Pius XII, St. John XXIII, St. Paul
VI, Venerable John Paul I, St. John Paul II, and many
others. Why not buy pizza and enjoy the food and great
movies! Have a family time and a family night! Let your
weekly plan of life build up your family!

- **Family Daily Mass**! A magnificent idea to really
  strengthen the family in the love of God and each
  other would be to choose an extra day of the week—in
  addition to Sunday—to attend Holy Mass and receive
  Holy Communion together. The bonds of family love
  and unity cannot be strengthened more than when the
  family receives Holy Communion together—the Body,
  Blood, Soul, and Divinity of Jesus Christ! Maybe a Friday night evening Mass to start off the weekend and to
  honor and make reparation to the most Sacred heart of
  Jesus for our sins and the sins of the whole world!

- **Book Reading and Idea Sharing**. How important it
  is to read and read and read. How much knowledge
  can be acquired through good and solid reading! How
  about this? Why not do this as a family? Once a week,
  set aside an hour in which the family can read a good
  book together, to strengthen the minds and fortify the
  hearts of all. Saint Philip Neri, founder of the Oratorian Fathers, had the habit of bringing friends together
  to pray, sing, read, reflect, and share. By carrying out
  this wonderful practice, all those of good will who were

involved in this group took leaps and bounds in their spiritual life! What would happen if families carried out this most noble enterprise? How much good knowledge could be acquired and shared, all in the context of the family which is the *Domestic Church!* Try it and you will reap abundant fruits. Add this to the list of your family weekly plan of life.

- **Invite a Poor Person to Your Table.** Although not a common practice, it is a biblical invitation. Why not invite a poor person to your table on a weekly basis, or if not weekly, every month. Jesus tells us not to invite the rich who can repay us, but the poor who have no means to repay us. By inviting the poor and marginalized, we are inviting the person of Jesus, and we will be richly rewarded on the day of our Judgment (Mt 25).

- **Weekly Holy Hour in the Family.** As an extension of our love for Jesus in the Holy Sacrifice of the Mass, why not go with your family to the church where the Blessed Sacrament is present, either in the tabernacle or exposed publicly in a monstrance, and make a family weekly Holy Hour. Jesus invites us: "Come to me, all who labor and are heavy laden, and I will give you rest" (Mt 11:28). May your family discover its true rest in the presence of Jesus in the most Holy Sacrament of the Altar!

- **Marian Day!** It has been a Catholic tradition to honor the Blessed Virgin Mary on Saturdays. There are many ways to honor Mary together as a family on Saturdays, such as reading a good book in her honor, praying the Rosary, praying the Litany of the Blessed Virgin Mary, fasting, renewing your consecration to Mary, or even attending Mass and receiving Holy Communion in her honor. Variety is the spice of life! Any of these can be utilized on Saturdays as part of your weekly family/ Marian plan of life!

So, we have come to the conclusion of our weekly plan of life, focusing on building up the family, which is the basic building block of society (Pope Saint John Paul II). By our concrete proposals, may we be ardent and fervent heralds of the salvation, sanctification, and restoration of the family as the heart of society! As the family goes, so goes the society!

8

DAILY PLAN OF LIFE

Much to Be Done in Twenty-Four Hours

IN our presentation of the plan of life we have gone from year to month, from month to week (focusing on many facets of the weekly block of time), and now we have arrived at trying to see how we can live out a daily plan of life. We continue to move from the general to the specific!

As mentioned earlier, *time is of the essence* in our brief earthly pilgrimage. The Psalmist reminds us of the transitory reality of life: "As for man, his days are like grass; he flourishes like a flower of the field; for the wind passes over it, and it is gone, and its place knows it no more" (Ps 103:15–16). Again, Saint James compares human life to a mere breath of smoke that disappears!

The famous Russian author Aleksandr Solzhenitsyn penned the classic *One Day in the Life of Ivan Denisovich.* In this Russian classic, the author goes through the hours and minutes that a prisoner of war spent in a concentration camp in Russia. The entire scope and arc of the day was explained in great detail. At lunch, to have the soup with the fat on the bone was seen as a real treasure! So it is with us: now it is time for us to look at the twenty-four hours of the day that God has given to us and be aware of the gift of these twenty-four hours, and how much we can return to Our Lord, good Master, and generous Benefactor!

It is not uncommon for individuals who have no compass, purpose, and direction in the short life that God has given to them to waste away a day, to do barely anything of lasting value. Worse yet, how many use their time for multiplying deeds of evil rather than actions that are pleasing to God and for the welfare of all of humanity.

Read Luke 16:19–31! In this parable, Jesus offers a marked contrast between Lazarus, the poor beggar outside the gate, and the rich man (sometimes called Dives) who dressed splendidly and feasted sumptuously. Upon their deaths the tables turned, and the rich man found himself tormented in fire while Lazarus was resting in Abraham's bosom. What was the reason for the condemnation of the rich man, Dives? He did not seem to be guilty of any sins of commission: lying, stealing, committing adultery, selling drugs, or causing wars! None of that comes to the surface! Then why the condemnation? Very simple: he was condemned not so much for what he did, *but for what he failed to do!* In other words, he was condemned due to sins of omission—not helping a poor man who desperately needed help. He failed to feed, to give drink, to clothe, to welcome, to show care and concern for a poor man, named Lazarus, who, as Christ tells us, was really Jesus in disguise! May

God grant us the grace to see Jesus present in the distress-
ing disguise of the poor (Saint Mother Teresa of Calcutta).

Therefore, let us move into our daily plan of life and pray
to the Holy Spirit for the light to see with the eyes of faith
what we can offer to the Lord every day of our lives.

Our Daily Offering to the Lord! Start off with Jesus
and Mary! Like Abel, we would like to offer to the Lord
our first-fruits, the best of our crops. Why not start every
day by praying the Morning Offering? Everything we say,
do, think, and even feel this day, we would like to offer as
a spiritual gift to Jesus through the hands and heart of the
Blessed Virgin Mary. We can never go wrong by giving
ourselves into the hands and Immaculate Heart of Mary.
Kiss the scapular. Hopefully, you are wearing *the Garment of Grace, the Scapular.* The Scapular of Our Lady of
Mount Carmel is our external sign of consecration to Jesus
through Mary. In conjunction with the Morning Offering,
you can also kiss the Scapular. By doing this small gesture
you are manifesting your love and confidence in Mary, and
your desire to please Jesus and Mary all twenty-four hours
of the day!

Daily Mass. Of all the actions that the human person can
accomplish, by far there is no comparison to that of attending the Holy Sacrifice of the Mass! The Dogmatic Consti-
tution of the Second Vatican Council expresses how we
should not be present at Mass as a mere passive spectator.
On the contrary, the document on the liturgy, *Sacrosanc-
tum Concilium*, exhorts those who go to Mass to participate

fully, actively, and consciously. Therefore, within the context of the Holy Sacrifice of the Mass, the reception of Holy Communion, which is truly and substantially the Body, Blood, Soul, and Divinity of Our Lord and Savior Jesus Christ, is the greatest action that a human person can do on earth! If at all possible, in writing out and living your daily plan of life, why not insert the intention of participating in Holy Mass and receiving Holy Communion daily as a high priority—better said, as the highest priority! The most famous prayer in the world is the Lord's Prayer that we commonly call *The Our Father*. In this prayer, composed of seven petitions, we pray *Give us this day our daily bread*. Could *daily bread* be interpreted as the reception of daily Holy Communion? I would give an absolute *yes* for those who have the time, effort, and good will. Often we fail to carry out our good intentions due to disorder in our lives. Once again, an essential part of our plan of life is to *order the disordered!*

Mealtime Prayer. For many years it has been a Catholic, as well as Christian, custom and tradition to start the evening meal by saying a prayer of blessing and thanksgiving for the food provided by God. Let us return to this habit if you have wandered away from it or never even had it! This can be done by praying the classical prayer: *Bless us, O Lord, and these thy gifts, which we are about to receive from thy bounty, through Christ our Lord. Amen.* Or, if you like, you can pray the Our Father: *Give us this day our daily bread.* Still another way is purchasing a series of biblical verse cards. Each night, a different short biblical passage is read by a member of the family, which can give a spiritual tone and theme to the meal, as well as become a source of family conversation at the table. Still yet, someone can even pray spontaneously. By doing this you invite Jesus to sit down at the meal with the family. What great company—in fact, the best!

Family Reading of the Bible. Another element that could be incorporated into the daily plan of life would be to form the habit of reading the Bible, the Word of God. This could be done in the context of the family and end with sharing and a prayer. Or it could be done individually. All of us should have hunger for the Word of God.

Daily Examen. Saint Ignatius of Loyola, who gave us the Spiritual Exercises, which is an excellent way to make a retreat, says that we should never allow a day to go by without making what he calls *The Daily Examen*. Indeed, this is an excellent prayer and it consists of five basic steps:

- **Beg for the Grace to Be Aware of God's Presence**. First, as Saint Augustine reminds us, *we are all beggars before God*. We beg God for the light to be aware of his presence.
- **Give Thanks to God**. Next, we give thanks to God for the blessings he has bestowed upon us during the course of the day. With the Psalmist, let us lift up our hearts: "Give thanks to the LORD, for he is good; for his steadfast love endures forever" (Ps 107:1).

- **Rewind the Day and Walk Through It With Jesus.** Then we rewind the day and walk through it with Jesus, keenly aware of his presence, love, and friendship during the hours, minutes, even seconds as we review the various events of the day and our response to them.

- **Repentance/Contrition.** Given that we were conceived in sin and are sinners up until our dying day, we must honestly and sincerely be aware of and admit times during our day when we flaunted God's grace by our pride, egotism, and selfishness. This we call sin! We want to be aware of the specific ways we sinned this day. We then express our sincere sorrow to the Lord and experience his merciful forgiveness. "A broken and contrite heart, O God, you will not spurn" (Ps 51:17).

- **Renewal.** Finally, the last step is that of looking into the future—the following day. Aware of our weakness, we ask the Lord for help in recognizing and avoiding the near occasions of sin tomorrow. Finally, we resolve to walk with the Lord, befriend the Lord, and love him all the days of our life!

The Psalms: A Daily Psalm! The most complete, as well as most beautiful and inspired prayer book in the world, is the Book of Psalms. There are 150 psalms in number. Most are attributed to King David who was inspired, of course, by the Holy Spirit. You might feel inspired to pray a psalm a day to keep the devil away!

Night Prayers. Of paramount importance for the family, as well as for every individual member of the family, is ending the day together talking to God, thanking God, and begging for his blessings for the future. *The family that prays together, stays together* (Ven. Father Patrick Peyton).

Family Blessings. It is true that the priest, whom we call *Father*, blesses the people, especially at the end of Holy Mass, or with the Blessed Sacrament at the end of Eucharistic Adoration. However, this does not negate the fact that parents can bless their children. In point of fact, parents should bless their children by their prayers, and by their good and holy example. But also, mom and especially dad—who should be the priest of the family—can and should bless their children. What a beautiful practice, indeed, after saying night prayers together, for the dad, the father, the priest of the family, to bless his children with the sign of the cross and then with Holy Water. All Catholic families should have Holy Water in their homes!

Thus, we have offered eight concrete proposals that we can offer to Jesus through the heart of Mary on a daily basis. Look into these proposals and choose what is within your means, what is possible or feasible for you. As mentioned earlier, it is of great value to work through your plan of life with the help of a competent spiritual director, who represents the Lord Jesus in our lives.

9

HOURLY PLAN OF LIFE

Our Hourly Offering to the Lord
Jesus—Powerful Hours!

WE have moved from year to month to week and now to the hour in composing our plan of life. Really, what we are aiming at in our life is to give all of our time to God so that he can use us in the way he desires. As Saint Teresa of Calcutta expressed it, we are called to be a pencil in the hands of God so he can write a beautiful story with us. So let us place ourselves, all that we are, and all that God wants us to be, like a ready pencil in the fingers and hands of God. Let us allow him to write the most beautiful poem, story, book with our lives!

Once again, we invite all to a spirit of magnanimity— great generosity in giving our total selves to God. "In him we live and move and have our being" (Acts 17:28). Let us give *all of our time* to God.

Like an eagle soaring above a beautiful mountain, let us gaze down and see the beauty of God's creation related to the precious time that he has given to us. Now it is through the lens or perspective of the hourglass! In days of old, time would be measured by the hourglass. Filled with sand, the hourglass would be turned on end and the grains of sand, slowly but surely, would drop from the upper part of the hourglass to the lower until it was totally emptied. So it is with us! We want to give ourselves totally to God the Father, as Jesus gave himself fully to the plan of God the eternal Father.

On one occasion, I was standing on a bridge contemplating the water that flowed rapidly beneath the bridge heading towards its destiny, a beautiful lake. As I contemplated the rushing water, the rippling waves, the utter beauty of the water, this thought penetrated my mind: the water that is flowing thus will never return again. It is likewise with time related to eternity. Once a minute has transpired, once an hour has finished, both are lost . . . forever. Every day that reaches midnight, terminates, never to return again for all eternity. As the poet declares: *Time is of the essence!* Therefore, in composing our hourly plan of life, in a true spirit of prayer and oblation, let us be keenly aware of the time that escapes us so quickly, like water running through our fingers.

Our Hourly Plan of Life

Upon Waking. Many are tempted by the devil from the very outset of the day; that is to say, from the moment they hear the alarm clock crowing like a rooster its morning wakeup call! The founder of Opus Dei, Saint Josemaria Escriva de Balaguer, coined the all-important phrase and concept of the *heroic moment*! What is this so-called *heroic moment*? Simply this: upon hearing the alarm clock ring, we can either stay in bed and hit the *snooze button* or dart out of bed to start the day. The Cure of Ars, Saint John Marie Vianney, says that those who start the day well will also finish well—as in racing to the finish line! We should interpret the alarm clock as the voice of God calling us to his most noble service for another day. Therefore, out of bed, like a dart, as soon as the alarm clock calls you! Note this in your daily plan of life.

The Heroic Moment. Yes, upon winning the battle of the *heroic moment*, get on your knees to pray your morning offering, in which you give yourself—all that you are, all that you possess, and all that you will do this da—to Jesus through the Immaculate Heart of Mary. The saints agree on this: devotion and love for Mary is the quickest, easiest, shortest, and most efficacious path to Jesus!

The Nine O'clock A.M. Hour: Pray the Angelus! A beautiful Marian prayer, highly recommended by the popes and the saints is the prayer of the Angelus. This prayer that the pope prays publicly at the Basilica of St. Peter on Sundays at noon is a brief Marian summary of the key moments in the history of salvation. The Angelus recalls the incarnation of the Son of God through the consent of Mary; it also calls to mind the Paschal Mystery—the passion, suffering, death, and resurrection of Jesus. Therefore, in our plan of life, why not propose to pray the Angelus every day at 9:00 a.m., or close to this morning hour, so as to sanctify the morning through the presence of the Blessed Virgin Mary. You can do this even at work in the silence of your heart. It will help you develop the constant habit of calling your mind to God if you have set prayers to say at set hours.

Twelve Noon: The Angelus Again. In the Philippines, a very Catholic country, it is a common phenomenon to pray the Angelus at noon and in a public and external fashion. By this we mean that even in public malls, stores, and supermarkets, at the chiming of the noon hour, all business stops and everybody prays the Angelus. After the Marian prayer is finished, business resumes. What a beautiful way to start the afternoon—with the presence and prayers of Mary, the Mother of God!

Three O'clock P.M.—The Chaplet at the Hour of God's Mercy! Jesus died on the cross for our eternal salvation on Good Friday at 3:00 p.m. This is what is termed *The Mercy Hour!* In the diary of Saint Faustina, *Divine Mercy in My Soul,* Jesus encourages Saint Faustina, as well as the world at large, to pray the Chaplet of Divine Mercy as often as possible. However, strongly encouraged by Jesus to Saint Faustina, and the whole world, is to pray the Chaplet of Divine Mercy daily at 3:00 p.m. This beautiful prayer, calling to mind the passion, death, and Precious Blood that Jesus shed for us on the cross, can be prayed publicly in the context of the family or privately by yourself. The chaplet can be prayed in front of the Blessed Sacrament in the church. It can be prayed in the *Domestic Church* which is the family. Or it can be prayed by you personally and privately in the quiet of your own room. Even if it happens to be that you are in your car driving to some destination, you can pray the Chaplet of Divine Mercy. Allow your car to be transformed into a mobile chapel-on-wheels! This prayer is very pleasing to Jesus. Also, with respect to economy of time, this prayer can truly be prayed in a few minutes.

Again, Three O'clock P.M.—The Mercy Hour. If it is such that you do not have the time or opportunity to pray the Chaplet of Divine Mercy at 3:00 p.m., then upon the request of Jesus to Saint Faustina, at 3:00 p.m. or close to the Mercy Hour you can at least lift up your mind and heart and unite it to the suffering and agonizing Jesus on the cross. Then Jesus says, beg for what you desire, and the Eternal Father cannot deny your request! A very important intention in the heart of the suffering Jesus is the conversion and salvation of sinners. Our Lady of Fatima stated that many sinners are lost because not enough people pray and sacrifice for them. Let us be generous with our time and good will so as to work with Jesus and Mary for the salvation of many immortal souls!

The Six O'clock P.M. Hour. Keeping with our Marian thread, why not pray the Angelus once again and now at 6:00 p.m.? By praying the Angelus at 9:00 a.m., again at 12:00 noon, then finally at 6:00 p.m., we end up by sanctifying the major blocks of our time with the presence of the Blessed Virgin Mary! If this is done, we give the morning, the afternoon, and finally the evening to Jesus through the *yes* of Mary! May the *yes* of Mary be our constant *yes*!

The Family Rosary: Choose the Best Hour! Venerable Patrick Peyton, known as *The Rosary Priest*, stated, *The family that prays together, stays together.* He also stated, *A world at prayer is a world at peace.* In his document *The Rosary and the Blessed Virgin Mary*, Pope Saint John Paul II urged all of humanity, but especially the family, to pray the most Holy Rosary to the Blessed Virgin Mary. The holy pontiff suggested praying the Rosary especially for two specific intentions: 1) For the sake of world peace (the document was written shortly after the attacks on Sept. 11, 2001); and 2) for the sake of the family, which is being attacked on all fronts! It helps to have a set time. A suggestion: why not have a fixed time to pray the most Holy Rosary right before the dinner mealtime. Another possibility is to make the Rosary part of your family nighttime prayers. To emphasize the power and need of praying the Rosary daily for peace in our families and our world, the Mother of God, Our Lady of Fatima is the one asking us to pray it daily! Let us recall the six appearances of the Blessed Virgin Mary to the three shepherd children of Fatima May 13 through October 13, 2017. At each appearance, Our Lady asked the children to pray the Rosary every day. Why? In honor of Our Lady of the Rosary and to obtain peace for the world. Were you aware that it was Our Lady herself who taught the children these words that we say in every Rosary: "When you pray the Rosary, say after each mystery: 'O my Jesus, forgive us our sins, save us from the fire of hell. Lead all souls to heaven, especially those most in need of Thy mercy.'" On Our Lady's last visitation, Lucia asked, "Will you tell me your name?" Our Lady responded, "I am the Lady of the Rosary." Form praying the Rosary as a habit in your family life, and Jesus, through the intercession of the Blessed Virgin Mary, will bless your family with incredible graces—peace, harmony, joy, purity of life and custom, and most especially eternal life!

Mealtime and Prayer. As mentioned in an earlier chapter, we should value the family mealtime. However, we should invite Jesus, Mary, and Saint Joseph to sit down at the table with us at mealtime, the meal hour, to share this quality time with our family. Do not forget to pray some prayer to bless the meal, but even more important, to bless the people sitting down for the meal. One family I know begins their meal by "saying grace" and then recites three Hail Marys. Are you familiar with the promises of the three Hail Marys?[1] My habit, when sharing a meal with friends, is that after the meal I say: *The food and meal was great, but the people with me even better!*

Every Hour Upon the Hour. If possible, you might make it a habit, through the help and inspiration of the Holy Spirit, to pray a short prayer upon the striking of every new hour. If this is done, you are sanctifying the start of this new hour that God has so generously given to you. This is a practice of some of the saints. These great friends of God—the saints—strove to live constantly in the presence of God. By living out our plan of life we will live more

---

[1]   See Appendix of Prayers for more information on this pious devotion.

and more in the presence of God—praying with more constancy, sinning less seriously and less frequently, and working more generously with God with fear and trembling for our eternal salvation and the salvation of many others! It can be any prayer of your choosing! However, maintaining our faithfulness to the Marian thread, why not pray the *Hail Mary*? To Mary, whom we call *Full of Grace*, why not beg for the grace every hour, by praying the Hail Mary, to be open to God's graces and inspirations for that hour!

Daily Examen Prayer. Every day find some time to do your daily Examen Prayer, the specifics of which were laid out for you in the previous chapter on the daily plan of life. Saint Ignatius insisted that under no circumstance whatsoever should this prayer be omitted! For this prayer helps us navigate through the hours of our day with the help of the Holy Spirit. Moreover, in living out our plan of life, let us be committed to having recourse to a spiritual director to ask for their light and input—an indispensable voice of the Holy Spirit in our life!

Night Prayers. We should never neglect praying our nighttime prayers. As a family unit, this is an incredible grace and blessing. If you are single or it is a challenge to bring everyone together in the evening due to homework or other commitments, everyone should do this at least on a personal basis. What prayers you might ask? Variety is the spice of life! You can pray any prayers, but there are classics or traditional prayers you can pray, and they are the following: The Our Father, Hail Mary, Glory Be, the prayer

to your Guardian Angel, and an Act of Contrition. Saint
Anthony of Padua and other saints strongly recommended
the praying of the three Hail Marys every night before retiring for the specific intention and purpose of purity through
the night. It is true that we desire to get a good night's rest,
but the devil never goes on vacation and he never rests.
One form of attack of the devil is that of attacks against the
virtue of purity in the night and sleeping hours. Therefore,
to overcome this insidious and insistent attack of the devil
of impurity, why not kneel before your bed and pray fervently the three Hail Marys to the most pure and Immaculate Heart of Mary for purity of mind, thought, eyes, body,
and intention at all times, but in a special way, during the
night hours! Also, do not forget to wear and to kiss your
scapular of Our Lady of Mount Carmel before retiring!

Any Hour or Place. We would be remiss if we did not
add *vigilance* to our hourly plan of life. St. Ignatius teaches
us to be constantly aware of our affective life—whether we
are in consolation or desolation. In consolation, we are
strong in faith, hope, and charity. We have wind in our
sails, energy to do good! In desolation, we are weak in faith,
hope, and charity. We lack motivation and energy to do
good, seeking creature comforts instead. We need to be
constantly aware of the condition of our heart, mind, and
soul—the consolation, to take advantage of the energy we
are experiencing; the desolation, to prepare for battle, for in
desolation the devil is our counselor! We need to have our
spiritual antennae raised on high to pick up the good vibes

and reject the bad vibes. As mentioned earlier, the devil never rests or goes on vacation. St. Peter says that the devil is like a roaring lion seeking whom he can devour. As part of your hourly program of life, you must be vigilant and on the alert for the state of desolation, mild or strong, that can strike you at any hour, and the inevitable attacks of the devil with his insinuations and lies! Your first recourse at any hour and place that the devil attacks you is to pray! Pray a *Hail Mary* to Mary, Terror of Demons! Pray and repeat the *name of Jesus*. Simply say the name of Our Lord. Pray the Jesus Prayer. "Lord Jesus Christ, Son of the living God, have mercy on me, a sinner." This practice will bring you a peace at all times and help you to "pray always." Invoke the Holy Family, "Jesus, Mary, and Joseph (also known as Terror of Demons) come to my assistance!" Follow up with the very powerful prayer to Saint Michael the Archangel! Have frequent recourse to this powerful archangel and prayer to fortify your defenses against the devil's assaults! It is a good idea to memorize it! A good soldier never goes into the field of battle without having his weapon at hand!

Your second recourse is to remain faithful to your daily prayers and the duties at hand, regardless of how you feel, especially when you don't feel like it! This is not hypocrisy; this is heroic virtue! Our good God will soon reward your heroic efforts—the darkness of the devil's lies and insinuations will begin to dissipate and the light of Christ's truth and promises shine forth! Your third recourse is to open up and discuss your state of desolation with your spiritual director, a confessor, or even a spiritual friend, as soon as possible! Why? Because the devil works in secret, in the dark. He tells you to keep your desolation to yourself, don't tell anyone—so he can make a mountain out of mole hill. As soon as you open up to someone, what seemed over-whelming begins to assume normal proportions and can be addressed or even dismissed!

Hourly Plan of Life: The Hour of Power—Ven. Fulton J. Sheen

Let us move into another possible integration in your hourly plan of life: the possibility of incorporating into your day a *Holy Hour* (not to be confused with the *Happy Hour*). Referring to the Holy Hour, Venerable Archbishop Fulton J. Sheen coined the phrase we referred to earlier: *The Hour of Power.*

At the end of his life, during that last stage after he retired as archbishop of the diocese of Rochester, New York, Sheen dedicated much of his time and energy towards the conver-sion, sanctification, and formation of priests by means of giving retreats. (Try listening to one of them on YouTube, for example the *Cor ad Cor*—meaning *Heart to Heart* with Jesus.) Sheen was a first-class master in the field of com-munication. One of the first radio evangelists in the coun-try, and one of the first televangelists in which millions of Americans would view and hear him speak every week, he moved the hearts of countless souls.

Archbishop, priest, and saintly apostle of the mass media

in the mid-twentieth century, Fulton Sheen believed firmly in the sanctification of priests and those who are endowed with the fullness of the priesthood, the bishops. Sheen had an invaluable weapon in his arsenal that he wielded and promoted among priests and bishops, especially in the context of the retreats that he gave to many of them.

The Hour of Power. Blunt and to the point in his retreat conferences, Sheen remarked that when many priests, as well as bishops, spoke, many of their listeners would turn a deaf ear; that is to say, ignore what they said. Whereas, when he opened his mouth to speak, all would listen! But why the difference? Point blank, Sheen asserted it was because he made a daily Holy Hour! This great modern priest and later archbishop, whose cause for canonization is in process, insisted upon this for both priests and bishops. Indeed, if they wanted to arrive at true conversion of heart and a deeper love of God, which would result in their increased ability to touch and move the hearts of their people to really love God, then the priests and bishops would have to make and keep the proposal of making a daily Holy Hour!

Sheen asserted with enthusiasm that if they made this proposal and would strive to be faithful to it, these priests and bishops would notice a remarkable change in their lives, and in the lives of those whom they ministered to on a daily basis! Sheen would point out at the very outset of the retreat that if they did not propose in their plan of life to make the daily Holy Hour, then he would consider the retreat to be a failure!

This holds true for laypeople like yourselves! You too must make a daily Holy Hour if you are to arrive at true conversion of heart and a deeper love of God which will touch and move the hearts of family, friends, and all those you encounter. If you incorporate this into your plan of life and faithfully practice the daily Holy Hour, there will be a remarkable change in your life and in the lives of those around you. For it is an immutable truth that when we change for the better, those around us change for the better as well.

This proposal for your plan of life might appear to be downright preposterous, absurd, or literally impossible! However, I would like to challenge you to take it on! My challenge is very simple, almost too simple! How many hours in the day? Obviously, twenty-four! Next, how much time do we end up wasting by pursuing superficial, frivolous activities? How much time do we simply waste? How much time do we spend in front of the TV, listening to the radio, browsing the Internet, texting or talking on the phone with friends, maybe even giving in to gossip? Being dead honest, many of us must admit in embarrassment and shame that there are blocks of time in our daily schedule that we simply waste! Given that life is so short, we really have no time to waste. As the saints remind us: we have all eternity to rest in heaven!

Now that hopefully we have convinced many of the utter

importance of the daily Holy Hour and of the reality that, if we are being truly honest with ourselves, it is possible to find time to do it, let us consider how we can actually carry out this most noble goal. Remember: it is only *one hour* out of a *twenty-four-hour* day! Indeed, a soap opera lasts an hour!

The actions of our life follow the convictions of our mind and heart! If indeed we are firmly convinced as to the importance of the daily Holy Hour, then we will find the time, the place, and exert the effort to carry it out! By the way, one of our best models in this regard is Archbishop Fulton J. Sheen himself; once he proposed to incorporate the daily Holy Hour into his plan of life as the first hour of his day, he never missed it once in more than fifty years as a priest, bishop, then archbishop.

The Nuts and Bolts of the Holy Hour!

Time! First of all, you must determine a set time of the day and try to be faithful to that set time. Men and women are creatures of habit. A bad habit is a vice; a good habit is a virtue. Why not establish in your life an incredibly good habit of prayer—the daily Holy Hour!

Be an Early Bird! We read in the first chapter of the Gospel of Saint Mark that Jesus got up way before dawn and he was absorbed in prayer. Take it as you like, *way before dawn!* We do not have the exact hour, but it was most clearly very early in the morning! This will set the tone for the rest of your day. Saint Faustina Kowalska noticed that when she put the Holy Hour off for a later time in the day, one of two things occurred: either she did not do it or she did it poorly. Imitate Abel rather than Cain and give the Lord your first fruits by giving him your first hour of the day as your Holy Hour.

Place! According to Sheen, his sacred place was in front of the most Blessed Sacrament, the Eucharistic Lord Jesus. For all of us, in front of the Blessed Sacrament is, of course, the ideal place. However, it may not be possible due to your living conditions. Therefore, in the quiet and silence of your own home, your domestic church, "make room" for Jesus; that is, establish a place.

Domestic Sanctuary. Create your own *domestic sanctuary*. As Catholics, we utilize images, paintings, statues, stained glass windows as a means by which we can arrive at the invisible God. This being said, to enhance your prayer experience and make an efficacious Holy Hour, you should create a spiritual milieu or atmosphere that will be propitious to meeting God. Therefore, you must create your own little domestic sanctuary, your own little place where you can encounter God. Images of Divine Mercy, the Sacred Heart of Jesus, the Immaculate Heart of Mary, Good Saint Joseph, other angels and saints can help us enter into our dialogue with God. In addition, the use of candles and aromatic, uplifting incense can also be a catalyst to catapult us to God in prayer.

Material for Prayer. To perform a Holy Hour, you should have some material to use for your meditation. Of the highest value of course would be the Bible, the Word of God, with preference for the Gospels. These are the means to connect you in a familiar dialogue with Jesus.

Prayer Method. To help you in your plan of life to live out the hour of prayer that we call the Holy Hour, it can be highly beneficial to have recourse to a particular prayer method. The following could be some concrete steps to fulfill this need in prayer: Place yourself in the presence of God. Imagine the face and eyes of Jesus looking at you with great love and compassion. Beg for the intercession of Mary to turn your water into wine. Beg for the help of the *Interior Master—the Holy Spirit*. He can teach you how to pray (Rom 8:26). Read from Scripture with the desire to connect with God. Beg: Speak, O Lord, for your servant is listening. Think about what God is saying to you. (Like Mary, who pondered the Word of God in her Immaculate Heart.) Open up your heart to God's action and allow affections to flow freely from your heart. What affections, you might ask? The following are a few: praise, adoration, admiration, wonder, awe, love, thanksgiving, remorse, contrition, oblation (giving of yourself to God), supplication—Augustine says that we are all beggars before God—and many other emotions. Talk to God from the depths of your heart using your own words. Be like a child in the arms of a loving mom or dad.

Revision. After you have finished your Holy Hour, write down in your journal or diary what were the inspirations, insights, consolations, messages that God gave you during the course of that hour. In living out your plan of life, when you visit your spiritual director, you can share with them what you have written. With their help, you will be able to discern what God is doing in your life and where he is moving you.

From Mind and Heart to Feet. Your deeper prayer life should affect the way you live and the way you treat and deal with other people. Consequently, your contemplative life should motivate you to be at the service of others, like the Blessed Virgin Mary who said *yes* to the Angel Gabriel in the Annunciation, and then was moved by the Holy Spirit to bring the joy of Jesus to her cousin Elizabeth who lived in the hill country.

Faithfulness. A key element for growth in your spiritual life is being faithful to God in living out your commitment to the daily Holy Hour as part of your plan of life. Saint Teresa of Avila, the Doctor of Prayer, put it in these words: "We should have a determined determination to never give up prayer." For this reason, meeting with a spiritual director is indispensable because of our human need for accountability for our actions; that accountability will help us remain faithful to our prayer exercises.

Transformation. By truly living out our plan of life and offering to God our daily Holy Hour, the Holy Spirit enters in a deeper way into our lives and gradually transforms us. A caterpillar turns into a butterfly, storm clouds dissipate manifesting God as painter in the gleaming and glimmering rainbow, and hard coal under pressure transforms into a beautiful diamond. Likewise, a great sinner can be transformed into a great saint inasmuch as he conforms himself to the life, the person, the words, the mind, and the heart of the Holy of Holies, the Lord Jesus Christ. In other words, the Holy Hour gradually transforms us so that we will be able to echo the words of the great apostle to the Gentiles, Saint Paul: "It is no longer I who live, but Christ who lives in me."

In conclusion, this important but challenging chapter invites all of us to humbly and sincerely examine the hours of our day with great magnanimity—meaning, great generosity of heart—and be ready and willing to give the Lord Jesus and Mary, his Mother and our Mother, an hour of prayer time every day. If we do this, then it is certain that this hour we call the Holy Hour—this hour we are willing to give from the twenty-four hours we have every day—will become our Hour of Power. This hour will empower us to walk with the saints and carry out marvelous works for the Lord and for the salvation of souls. Are you willing to accept the challenge?

If sixty minutes reading and praying with Scripture seems intimidating to begin with, start with thirty minutes with the firm purpose and resolve to increase to sixty minutes once your habit of daily reading and praying with Scripture is established. Jesus himself gave us this model of prayer in the Garden of Gethsemane when he said to his disciples, "So, could you not watch with me one hour? Watch and pray that you may not enter into temptation."

Then Jesus said, "The spirit indeed is willing, but the flesh is weak" (Mt 26:40–41). Beg our Blessed Mother Mary and the Holy Spirit to give you strength and a determined determination to give the Lord one hour a day, and he will bless the other twenty-three hours, for he is faithful and cannot be outdone in generosity!

10

EVERY MINUTE PLAN OF LIFE

How We Can Give Our Minutes
to God—All Is the Lord's

IF we are really humble and honest, we must admit that
all that we have in our lives, with the exception of our
sins (that we have freely chosen), are gifts from an all loving
and generous God.

The family we're born into, health, intelligence, money,
opportunities, talents, wit and charm, communication
skills, musical, artistic or athletic ability, even the faith that
we have in a Supreme Being whom we call God—all of
these are sheer gifts from God that we have not merited to
receive because of any innate goodness in ourselves.

Let us move into another area of our plan of life and
beg for the grace to be aware of even the minutes that God
has given to us, and the importance of utilizing even this
smaller bracket of time for his honor and glory. As Saint
Paul reminds us, quoting a Greek poet: "In him we live and
move and have our being" (Acts 17:28).

The major thrust of this chapter that deals with minutes is to help us realize how much good can be done, with

91

respect to a well-cultivated prayer life, even in the space of a single minute. Since another positive fruit of the plan of life is to recognize that our life on earth is indeed very short—as Saint James reminds us, our life is a mere puff of smoke—then we should take advantage of all the opportunities that we have in life to constantly draw closer to God.

This being said, let us step back and pray for a keen awareness of the essence of prayer and how much good we can do in the shorter segments that God so generously offers to us.

Time to Pray to God—Prayer, the Oxygen of Our Soul!

The Hail Mary. A prayer that is most pleasing to the Blessed Virgin Mary—in which her heart rejoices upon hearing the words "Hail, Mary, full of grace"—can be prayed in a matter of thirty seconds or even less. However, its value is worth more than all of the gold in the world!

The Angelus. This beautiful Marian prayer consists of three Hail Marys, with a short prayer in between the Hail Marys, and a closing prayer. This prayer can be prayed in three to four minutes. In it we recall the incarnation of the Son of God, as well as his passion, death, and resurrection—the Paschal Mystery; all with the presence of Mary.

The Litanies of the Blessed Virgin and Sacred Heart Of Jesus. These prayers consist of a series of poetic, mystical, and inspiring phrases, some taken from the Bible, others from the saints or mystical poetry. Often a litany is prayed after the Holy Rosary and can be prayed in five minutes. Add this to your plan of life.

The Chaplet of Divine Mercy. This beautiful prayer that Jesus taught Saint Faustina Kowalska and that can be found in her classic diary, *Divine Mercy in My Soul*, can be prayed in five minutes. Of course, the Mercy Hour is 3:00 p.m. However, Jesus encouraged Saint Faustina—as well as us—to pray it often. If you have five free minutes driving on the freeway, waiting in line at the grocery store, waiting for someone at the train station, or simply five free minutes, then pull out your Rosary beads and pray the Chaplet of Divine Mercy. Immortal souls can be saved by this short but powerful prayer!

The Most Holy Rosary. The prayer that fills the heart of the Virgin Mary with overflowing joy is the Most Holy Rosary. Give yourself fifteen to twenty minutes and you will have prayed a Rosary!

All Four Mysteries of the Rosary. There are fervent Catholics with a great love for the Blessed Virgin Mary who throughout the course of the day pray the Rosary four times—meditating on the Joyful, Luminous, Sorrowful, and Glorious Mysteries—in about an hour or an hour and twenty minutes. How pleasing to the Blessed Virgin Mary is the prayer of the Most Holy Rosary. Pray it and promote it as part of your plan of life.

A Psalm a Day Keeps the Devil Away! Go to your Bible and get in the habit of praying a Psalm every day! There are 150 in total. Before retiring at night, you could read and pray one of the 150 Psalms. Without a doubt, it is the most inspired prayer book ever composed, whose author is the Holy Spirit. You can pray a Psalm in a matter of a few minutes, if not less! However, if you feel inspired to go deep, you can spend hours meditating upon the Psalms. Be led by the Holy Spirit!

Daily Holy Mass. Of course, the greatest prayer that exists is the Holy Sacrifice of the Mass. We have already made reference to Holy Mass and Holy Communion; once again in this scheme of minutes, we invite you to look at your schedule to see if you can fit daily Holy Mass into your schedule. If at all possible, you will never regret daily Mass and daily Holy Communion. *Give us this day our daily Bread!*

Visit to the Blessed Sacrament. There is a short, easy to memorize poem that summarizes this point: *Whenever I see a church, I stop to make a visit; so that when I die the Lord won't say, "Who is it?"* If you are driving and pass by a Catholic church that has its doors open, then the Sacred Heart of Jesus is open to you! Why not make a short visit? Even if your visit is nothing more than three to five minutes, this can be very pleasing to Our Lord. What should you do? Enter the church where Jesus is truly present in the tabernacle. Make a reverential genuflection. Pray this short Eucharistic prayer: "O Sacrament most holy, O Sacrament Divine, all praise and all thanksgiving be every moment thine." Then, as is the custom among friends, talk to Jesus like a little child. Jesus said: "Unless you turn and become like children, you will never enter the kingdom of heaven" (Mt 18:3). Tell Jesus how you feel and what is on your mind—your plans, worries, hopes, fears, anything you so desire. Then end with the Hail Mary.

Fifteen Minutes with Jesus in the Blessed Sacrament. If you are in no hurry, there is no reason why you cannot extend your short, few minutes visit into fifteen minutes, or even more. There is a small booklet—a real gem, a real treasure—with the title *Fifteen Minutes*. It is designed to help us cultivate an ever-deeper relationship of friendship with Jesus the Lord. Purchase it and use it with your Eucharistic visits!

So, friends, we have terminated our unique chapter on the value of minutes and how we can value these prayers, these treasures, in the space of just a few minutes! Never forget the real value of prayer: *What oxygen is to our lungs, so is prayer to our soul!*

We left for last how we can give even the *seconds* of our day to the Lord. How? Make the intention when you rise each day and retire each night that your every heartbeat is saying: "Jesus and Mary, I love you. Glory to the Trinity!"

PART 3

PROFESSIONAL AND VOCATIONAL PLAN OF LIFE

11

WHAT IS THE PROFESSIONAL AND VOCATIONAL PLAN OF LIFE?

Purity of Intention

DO the ordinary with extraordinary love!

Variety is the spice of life. This saying can be applied to the variety of ways that we can compose our plan of life. We have already proposed the chronological plan of life in which we presented breaking down our spiritual life into blocks of time, then writing or composing certain acts of piety, penance, or specific prayers that we could incorporate into our lives yearly, monthly, weekly, daily, hourly, even down to using our minutes so as *to order the disorder* in our lives.

Plan of Life: My Profession and Vocation

Now we would like to introduce you to another form, manner, or angle that you can use to compose your plan of life. We can title this plan of life professional or vocational. Our sanctification, our growth in holiness, and the realization of God's plan for us depends in large part on our being faithful to our own specific profession and vocation. Then we must strive to carry out our daily duties or obligations with *purity of intention*, and this combined with energy and exertion!

One of the most famous modern saints is Saint Thérèse of Lisieux, known commonly as *the Little Flower*. In her short life, which lasted only twenty-four years, this contemplative and cloistered Carmelite nun did nothing out of the ordinary. No miracles were attributed to her during the course of her life. Her exterior actions did not seem to be stupendous, sparkling, or even outside the course of the normal and mundane actions of convent life. However, there was indeed something in her life that she excelled in, more than most of us, and it was this: she did the ordinary tasks of her daily life with extraordinary love! That was the key and the secret to her *Little Way* that has become a modern model for arriving at true holiness. Saint Paul reminds us of this with these simple but profound words: "Whether you eat or drink, or whatever you do, do all for the glory of God" (1 Cor 10:31).

On one occasion, Jesus was in the entrance of the Temple of Jerusalem observing people deposit their money in the metallic collections box. Some threw in huge sums of coins that would resound throughout the Temple so that all would be aware of the quantity by the loudness of the dropping of the offering. Jesus did not pay too much attention to these rich, vain, and pompous individuals. Then a poor widow entered the Temple. Being poor, she could offer nothing more than two copper coins—a few pennies and not much more. This was the person that Jesus exalted and praised among the givers. Why? The others gave out of their abundance, whereas this poor widow gave of her livelihood, all that she had. And for all time and eternity, this poor widow will be praised. This can be applied to us! We may not have too much to give economically. We may not be millionaires. We may not have huge bank accounts which we can delve into and dole out by the thousands! However, there is something that we can do in imitation of the poor widow; we can give generously from what we do have as a gift from God.

On one occasion, the great English convert Saint John Henry Newman was asked how to be holy, if you like, *a recipe for holiness!* Perhaps surprisingly, these were the practical daily points to grow in holiness given by this great man of God:

- Get to bed on time! Importance of a good night's rest!
- Upon rising, offer your first thoughts to God—the Morning Offering!
- Eat and drink to the honor and glory of God. Sounds like Saint Paul: "Whether you eat or drink, or whatever you do, do all for the glory of God" (1 Cor 10:31).
- Banish bad thoughts immediately! Keep the enemy outside!
- Make a good visit to the Blessed Sacrament. Love Jesus in the Eucharist!

- Pray the Rosary! Honor the Blessed Virgin Mary by praying the prayer that she loves most—the Most Holy Rosary.
- Finally, and of paramount importance: do the ordinary things of your daily life with extraordinary love.

Here you have it, a very simple daily plan of life from a convert to Catholicism, a scholar, a lover of truth, and a practical lover of God. His suggestions are not beyond comprehension or beyond our ability. On the contrary, these suggestions and advice can be followed by almost all of us!

The essence of the message of this chapter is to arrive at the humble recognition that God does not pay so much attention to exterior actions and the applause one might receive, or the recognition and praise that others may give. Rather, God reads the heart. We pay keen attention to appearances; God, on the contrary, pays attention to the heart, and even the most secret intentions of the heart. Remember how God sent the Prophet Samuel to the house of Jesse and his sons? The strong, tall, handsome, and impressive sons were discarded. It was the last in line, the humble shepherd of the sheep in the fields, David, who was called, chosen by God and anointed by Samuel to be God's king. What man considers great, God despises; what man considers of little or no value, God esteems most highly!

So it is with us! We may not have much to give, but God receives most willingly from a pure heart, a generous heart, a detached heart, a humble heart. God can multiply beyond our wildest imagination the small things that we give with great love. Call to mind how the little boy offered Jesus all he had—five loaves and two fish. Jesus was so pleased by this small offering given with such great generosity that he multiplied the loaves and the fishes so that thousands could be fed! Now it is up to us to look into our lives and see what we can do to change and give more generously to God, with a pure heart, and with nobility of intention.

Having set the stage by emphasizing the primary importance of purity of heart and purity of intention in all of our actions, even if they seem to be most insignificant, let us proceed in the next chapters to learn how in concrete we can compose a *professional and vocational plan of life* by living out our profession and our vocation to the fullest extent possible.

12

MARRIAGE AND FAMILY LIFE

IN this different perspective or angle in choosing and living out a plan of life, the focus is on listing different areas of the vocation of marriage and then examining these areas with great sincerity, humility, and honesty, and admitting there is still need for a lot of improvement.

Only God is perfect and we are all *perfectible beings*. The first message of Jesus in his public ministry was: "The kingdom of God is at hand; repent, and believe in the gospel" (Mk 1:15). Following up once again on one of the basic threads and themes of our work, with the help of Saint Ignatius of Loyola, we would like to strive to *order the disordered* in our lives so as to praise God more fully and work generously for our sanctification and the salvation of a multitude of souls!

This being said, let us point out areas to be worked on, to be improved for our growth in holiness in marriage.

Vocation as Spouse: Husband or Wife

Here are ways in which you can improve in your relationship with the spouse God has given to you, calling to mind the words solemnly professed on your wedding day:

"I promise to be faithful to you in good times and in bad, in health and in sickness, in riches and in poverty, until death do we part." This solemn promise was made before God and the praying community. The following are a list of areas worthy of reflection and examination of conscience:

- **Time**. Can I spend more time with my spouse? Time is of the essence; particularly time spent with my spouse!
- **Communication**. Time is important, but equally important is that of communication—time spent simply talking with my spouse without interruptions. Can I improve in this area?
- **Admiration**. Do I admire my spouse and tell him/her how much I really do admire him/her?
- **Affection**. Do I manifest my affection for my spouse by gestures like a hug, a kiss, or a caress? Or have I become cold and calloused over time?
- **Shared Activities**. Have I become distant and fail to work, recreate, and collaborate with my spouse to build the marriage that we promised to construct?

Vocation as Parent: Mother or Father

By choosing the married state, both husband and wife say *yes* to having children, to cooperating with God in bringing new life into existence. However, having children is not simply to engender and bring forth physical life and existence—even the animals do that much! In hammering out your vocational and professional plan of life, you must step

back like an eagle hovering over a vast landscape and see
the areas of your parenting that are good. However, part of
the professional and vocational plan of life is improvement,
conversion, and a humble admission that there is still much
to be done. All families in which parents are at work raising children, especially teens, are a *work in progress!* What
then might be practical points for improvement in your
parenting?

- **Time.** As is in the case of the relationship between
  spouses with respect to time, equally important is the
  concept of time with respect to parents and their relationship with their children. Parents have to make time
  to be with their children. This cannot be neglected!
- **Presence.** Parents must be present to their children, but
  a total presence: physical, mental, emotional, moral,
  and spiritual. Work at improving your living *presence*
  with your children.
- **Play with Them.** Pope Francis in dealing with married
  couples will sometimes ask them: *How much time do
  you play* with your children. For children, the first level
  of dialogue and communication can be that of play.
  Playing produces joy, bonding, harmony, warmth, and
  love. Find time to play with your children. Write this
  out in your plan of life!
- **Talk to Your Children.** In a world in which social and
  electronic media dominates so much time and so many
  places, parents must discover, cultivate, and defend
  blocks of time in which they talk with their children

and help them talk with one another! This can be done with all of your children as a group or family. Topics can be what they're learning in school, their other activities such as sports or recitals, funny (or not-so-funny) things that happened that day, or a good and clean joke, even current events. Family dinner time is a great time to have these conversations. Fond and lasting memories are created at such times. Add this to your plan of life!

- **Talk to Them Individually**. Parents should periodically make time to have a friendly talk with their children individually. When a child has a one-on-one conversation with mom or dad, they feel their self-importance, their self-worth, and their value. This is also an opportunity for their individual needs and concerns to surface and be lovingly addressed. Find time in your busy schedule to talk with each of your children. Mark it on your plan of life!

- **Pray with Them**. The famous Father Peyton's slogan rings true in the family structure: *The family that prays together, stays together.* Do you make time every day to pray with your children? Do you pray the family Rosary? Do you say family night prayers? If your response is a resounding no, then add these or some variant thereof to your plan of life! Parents must pray for their children, teach their children to pray, and pray with their children. Prayer is of paramount importance for the salvation of your soul and the souls of your children!

As well as for the salvation of the whole world, which starts with the Domestic Church—the local family!

- **Loving Your Children.** Many times, children never hear from their parents these words: *I love you!* Do not feel bashful or ashamed to say those three very important words to your children: *I love you!* When all is said and done, what everybody in the world wants to hear, feel, and relish within the depths of their hearts is that they are loved, by God and by their loved ones—*especially their parents!*

- **Correcting Your Children.** A few years ago, Pope Benedict XVI wrote a Lenten letter, a message to the whole Church and the world at large, on the primary importance of expressing love and concern through the art of what is called *fraternal correction. Yes, fraternal correction is a dimension of love!* What this means is simply this: if parents observe that their children are choosing the wrong path, making wrong decisions, following wrong directions and indications, then as an act of love the parents should intervene and make corrections! If we notice a house is on fire, we call the fire department! If a vicious animal is on the loose, we cry wolf! If there is a steep precipice around the bend, we cry out: danger ahead; drive carefully! With even more energy and exertion this should be the case in directing one's children on the path that leads to eternal life!

Thus far, we have explored two areas of analyzing our professional and vocational plan of life related to the vocation of marriage: our relationships with our spouse and with our children. The plan of life is designed to help us to *order the disordered*, to improve in our personal lives, our moral lives, and our spiritual lives for our own sanctification and perfection, but also for the welfare of our family and loved ones! In the following chapters, we will continue looking at our plan of life related other to areas in our lives that we can work on with goodwill and generosity!

13

OUR WORK LIFE

L ET us continue on our journey in our plan of life composition utilizing another scheme: that of looking at
the work or profession that you carry out, and beg for the
grace from God to improve, or if you like, to *order the disordered* in your life!

We have already shone the spotlight on two aspects to be
examined in the life of a married couple—your relationship
with your spouse and the relationship that you have with
your children. We offered some points on how you might
upgrade these relationships!

Therefore, it is time to dig deeper into other areas of
your life to see the possible decay, decomposition, and dead
wood that must be removed, cut out, severed; for as Jesus
tells us in the image of the Vine and the Branches (Jn 15),
you must bring forth fruit and fruit in abundance.

At Work

All of us are called to work. After the sin of our first parents, Adam and Eve, God told Adam that he would earn
his bread by the sweat of his brow (Gn 3). Saint Benedict,
the Patron of Europe and Western monasticism, coined

this phrase: *Ora et Labora*—meaning, *Pray and Work*. This should be the motto of all the followers of Christ. We must pray frequently and fervently, filled with faith. Furthermore, our prayers should overflow into our work world. This being said, let us highlight some areas with respect to improving our work ethic.

- **Laziness.** Do you consider yourself lazy? Where would you put yourself on a scale from zero to ten—with zero being not at all lazy and ten being lazy to the max? Laziness militates against all our efforts, especially successful work. Remember, we have one life, our life is short, and one day we will have to go before the judgment seat of God. We don't want to go empty-handed, do we?

- **Late/Never Punctual.** Are you the type of person who arrives late for everything? For school, work, Mass, appointments, obligations? Hopefully you will not arrive too late after the gate of heaven has been locked and bolted! Add this to your plan of life: punctuality, especially with regard to your work hours!

- **Cutting Corners.** Are you the type of person who works but cuts corners, or does the work half-hearted, or does an incomplete job—in a word, a sloppy worker? Never forget that your real boss is the Lord Jesus. We want to give him our best, not the left-overs and crumbs!

- **Chitter-Chatter—Gossip!** Is your work, or break, or lunch time characterized by useless and even harmful chitter-chatter or gossip? A sober reminder: all of the useless and harmful words that issue from our mouth will be subject to judgment before the Lord Jesus, who will come to judge the living and the dead.

- **Methodical, Organized, and Systematic!** These three words should be the hallmarks of your work ethic! Work must have a method. Also, organization is of indispensable value in efficacious work. Finally, work should be systematic—consistent with your goals. The saints lived lives motivated by these work facets! So should you!

- **Gratitude.** Do you suffer from the modern sickness or malady called *complainitus!* Why complain about your work? At least you have work, which many would love to have. Remember the words of the poet: *I complained because I had no shoes, until I met somebody who had no feet.* There are always those who are worse off than you. Cultivate an attitude of gratitude with respect to your work.

- **Workshops/Seminars for Growth or Improvement.** Maybe it is such that your work has become stale and you are in the pit or doldrums of mediocrity. Maybe it is time to attend a workshop or seminar to update and upgrade your work efficacy and interest? Sign-up and off you go! Add professional or occupational improvement and development to your plan of life.

At Home

We can never overestimate the great value of a mom (and, though less common, a dad) who is at home dedicated to the most noble task of being a homemaker. Indeed, this can be taxing and demanding! It requires hard work, dedication, patience, perseverance, in a word, much love for God and for the family! This being said, let us analyze and examine how we might improve on our work in the home—the family—the Domestic Church!

- **Cleanliness Is Next to Godliness.** This proverb has truth, but it is not always easy. Can you homemakers attest to the fact that your home is spotless and immaculate on a daily basis? Probably not! Maybe some improvement can be done in this area?
- **Washing.** How about the washing and ironing of clothes so important for your family members? Years ago, there was no such thing as a washing machine. Now it is in continual use. Are your family's clothes ready for wearing? Or maybe you drag your feet in this area?
- **Cooking.** If you are a homemaker, then you are also a cook. Maybe you would not be hired as the head chef at a five-star restaurant, but how would you rate your cooking skills? Do you just throw things on the table at the last moment? Or do you labor and strive to make better meals for your family? Call to mind the words of Jesus: "I was hungry and you gave me food, I was thirsty and you gave me drink. . . . As you did it to one of the least of these my brethren, you did it to me" (Mt 25:35, 40).

- **Buying**. Do you buy what is best for your family, what is necessary for your family? Or might it be the case that you buy superfluous things that are not really needed? This too is part of being a homemaker, a mother, and a daughter of the eternal Father. How easy it is to be swept away by materialism and allow our possessions to take possession of us!

- **Welcoming**. How about your *welcoming ministry*? Is your home cheery, welcoming, inviting, cordial, hospitable? In a word, are your homemaking skills such that all those who enter your home experience a warm and affectionate welcome, like Jesus who was welcomed into the home of Mary, Martha, and Lazarus in Bethany?

Thus, we come to the conclusion of another chapter in our professional and vocational plan of life. Work is part and parcel of our human existence. All of us must work. We should view work as a blessing. We should see work as a way to collaborate with God. Work is meant for our own perfection. Also, work well done and with purity of intention is a most necessary means to promote the common good and the growth and development of the human family! *Ora et Labora*—let us pray fervently, but also work hard! Saint Paul challenges us: "Work out your own salvation with fear and trembling" (Phil 2:12).

14

OUR SOCIAL RELATIONSHIPS

THE poet John Donne expresses the importance of social relationships stating, "No man is an island entire of itself." Aristotle stated, "Man is by nature a social animal." And of the greatest importance is the example of Jesus. He chose twelve apostles whom he called his *friends.* Of these twelve, Jesus had an inner circle of *best friends,* and they were three: Peter, James, and John. Then of the three, there were two *best friends:* Peter and John. Finally, of the two, Jesus's *best and most intimate friend* was the beloved disciple John! To John, the greatest of all of his friends, Jesus would give his Mother as he died on the cross: "'Woman, behold, your son!' Then he said to the disciple, 'Behold, your Mother!' And from that hour the disciple took her into his own home" (Jn 19:26–27).

Now it is incumbent upon us in the panoramic overview of our life to analyze in great detail our social relationships, which consist most likely of both relatives and friends. To do this, we must first understand this timeless truth of Saint Ignatius of Loyola in the Spiritual Exercises no. 23, "Principle and Foundation: Man is created to praise, reverence, and serve God our Lord, and by this means save his soul.

The other things on the face of the earth are created for man to help him in attaining the end for which he is created."

Definition of Friend

There are many definitions that we can give to the word *friend*. The great Greek philosopher Aristotle defined friends as those who share a commonality of interests. We would venture to offer another definition related to *Principle and Foundation*, which means seeing a friend in the light of our eternal destiny—arriving safe and sound in our eternal home, heaven. Jesus is our best friend who helps us achieve the end for which we were created, heaven! Therefore, considering the other persons in our life, we would define a friend as such: *Someone who helps us to draw deeper in friendship with Jesus, the best of all friends.* In other words, this definition of friendship is directly related to our friendship with Jesus and our eternal destiny to be with him forever in heaven. If the person that I call *friend* jeopardizes, hurts, wounds, damages, or worse yet, ruptures or severs my relationship with Jesus, then it is a pseudo-friendship; that is to say, a false friendship—not really a friendship at all!

This being said, let us enter into the plan of life for our social relationships—let us study, analyze, and examine each one to see if it is a true friendship, or a friendship that should be cooled, or a pseudo-friendship that should be ended once and for all!

My Social Relationships: Applicable to Friends and Relatives

Step Back and Look: Eagle's View! Step back and observe all your social contacts, but try to view them through the divine perspective, through the eyes of God, the Father of all.

Bad Contacts. Being dead-honest and sincere, in the presence of Jesus, Mary, the angels, and the saints, ask yourself if there are contacts—be it relatives or so-called friends—who are truly jeopardizing or damaging your relationship with Jesus, who is really your *best friend.*

End Them! Even though this may appear somewhat extreme, as well as exceedingly difficult, Jesus might be challenging you to cut, sever, and end those relationships. If some person, whom you call *friend,* is hurting your *friendship with Jesus,* why wouldn't you take the drastic measure of ending that friendship once and for all!

Less Time and Energy. Then there might be a middle-ground experience or relationship. By this we mean a friendship with a person who is noble, good, spiritual, with high ideals and pursuits like yours. However, the time you spend with this person is extreme. It is too much! Because of the time spent on the phone or over coffee with your friend, you are aware, due to this examination, that you are neglecting your time with God, with your spouse, with your children, and with other aspects of your life that need attention. Conclusion? This is not a call to end this friendship, but a call to moderate it; that is to say, give less time and energy to this social relationship.

A New Contact: Upgrade Your Social Life. Or the reverse may be true. Maybe it has happened that there is a person—in some parish group or setting—whom you believe is holy, dedicated, hardworking, prayerful, and inspiring, with many other virtues. After talking with them several times, you realize that each time you leave filled with spiritual consolation and peace. This could be Jesus, your best friend, speaking through this inner consolation that he wants you to expand your horizons and establish a friendship with this person. Remember the initial definition of a true friend—someone who helps us get closer to Jesus, our best friend! The Old Testament states that encountering a true friend is a treasure—a pearl of infinite value in our social life.

In conclusion, step back and beg the Holy Spirit for true insight to see the quality and caliber of those you associate with in your social life. Most likely God is challenging you in one of these three ways: to cut a relationship, moderate a relationship, or possibly cultivate a new friendship, always with the purpose of growing in friendship with your three best friends: Jesus, Mary, and Saint Joseph!

15

PERMANENT INTELLECTUAL FORMATION IN THE FAITH

IN all worthy professions, there is a need to work on a constant program of formation. Doctors, lawyers, teachers, engineers, architects, priests—all must be engaged in a process of permanent formation. This concept must apply also to those who take their Catholic faith seriously. Learning only stops in death.

Therefore, in the composition of our professional and vocational plan of life, we should stop and ask ourselves this all-important question: *Am I really growing in the knowledge of my Catholic faith, or am I stagnant?*

Jesus stated that the greatest of all commandments is to love God with all your heart, *mind*, soul, and strength, and then to love your neighbor as yourself (Lk 10:27). Let us now address the topic of our plan of life with respect to the project of our plan of studies.

Progress in Our Plan of Studies

The Bible. The great Saint Jerome asserted, "Ignorance of the Sacred Scriptures is ignorance of Christ." In your plan of life, find some time to read, study, and learn the Bible so you can put it into practice in your life. Indeed, may the Bible become the rule and guide of your life!

Catechism of the Catholic Church. One of the most important and authoritative Church writings in the past several decades is the *Catechism of the Catholic Church*, published during the pontificate of Pope St. John Paul II under the supervision of Cardinal Joseph Ratzinger (the future Pope Benedict XVI). As a tool for growth in the knowledge of our Catholic faith, reading this is a must!

The Lives of the Saints. If we want to see the life of Jesus lived out in concrete, everyday circumstances throughout history, then we should get into the habit of reading the lives of the saints. These were God's faithful friends in their lives on earth, and now they are God's friends in heaven for all eternity! The Catechism says the saints can help us in two ways: 1) Intercession—they can pray and intercede for us before the throne of God with their powerful prayers; 2) Example—their example of virtue is a powerful motivation for us to follow in their footsteps. They encourage us to *be holy as our heavenly Father is holy* (see Mt 5:48).

Catholic Television. One of the most powerful means of communication for Catholic information is Catholic television. Of enormous success, spreading throughout the English-speaking world and now even the Spanish speaking world, is EWTN—Eternal Word Television Network. The founder of this spectacular Catholic news and education media was a contemplative Franciscan nun, Mother Angelica. If you can find time to view some of the

programs on this network, it will be a powerful and efficacious means to flourish and blossom in the formation and
knowledge of your Catholic faith. Check it out; try it! You
will not regret it!

Catholic Talk Radio Stations. Not only can we use
Catholic television as a tool for our ongoing formation,
but we can also listen to Catholic talk radio stations. There
are a number of good Catholic radio stations around the
country, and with the internet, you should be able to easily
find if one is available in your area. Good Catholic radio
features content that is in harmony with the magisterial
teachings of the Catholic Church and the teachings of the
papacy. Catholic talk radio stations are important for many
reasons; one of the most obvious being that many people
commute and spend a good amount of time in their car, or
on a bus, train, or subway. Why not transform your car (or
chosen means of transportation) into a portable chapel and
Catholic learning center by tuning into instructive, inspiring, and encouraging Catholic programs?

Conferences, Lectures, Seminars, Congresses. Over
the past fifty years in most American cities, Catholic conferences, lectures, seminars, and congresses on the Catholic
faith have been launched covering a whole series of topics.
Keep your ears open and eyes peeled to catch such opportunities. As you become aware of them, try to incorporate
these programs into your plan of life.

Catholic Book Clubs and Sharing. From the great
genius of Saint Philip Neri, founder of the Oratorian

Fathers, came the organization of reading groups. How did this originate? Very simple! Saint Philip would encourage a relatively small group of people who had a real hunger for God to come together. He would encourage the group to first pray for the presence of the Holy Spirit. Next, they would read together some spiritual text. Then, moved spontaneously by the Holy Spirit, any person in the group could share the spiritual insight given to them by the Holy Spirit, thus enriching the other members in the group. After this sharing, another member would be inspired to do the same. In this way all the members who felt inspired and motivated by the Holy Spirit would share according to the promptings of the Holy Spirit. At the end, they would sing a song. All the members would return to their homes filled with greater knowledge of God, greater love for God, and a deeper community spirit. Today this movement of the Holy Spirit can be seen in the Catholic book clubs that are sprouting up throughout the country. Does your parish have one? If not, maybe you are called to start one? Maybe this can be an addition to your plan of life. No doubt this can be a valuable tool to increase your knowledge and love of God!

So we have concluded our professional and vocational plan of life on permanent intellectual formation. As a concluding note, we strongly encourage parents to take seriously this concept of *permanent intellectual formation* in their spiritual life. No one can give what they don't have! Indeed, if parents are the primary educators of their children—especially in the realm of faith—how important it really is for parents to be constantly learning their faith so as to keep growing deeper in their faith and their love of God! The beneficiaries? Of course, it will be the children of these well-educated, well-formed parents! However, what applies to parents, applies to all of us! We are all called to spread the Gospel! May Our Lady, under the title *Seat of Wisdom,* pray for us that we have an ardent yearning and longing to grow in our faith and share it with others!

16

CALL TO THE APOSTOLATE

IN the *Spiritual Exercises of Saint Ignatius of Loyola*, the saint presents a powerful contemplation—*The Call of the Temporal King so as to hear the Call of the Eternal King* (*Spiritual Exercises*, no. 91). The grace that Ignatius invites us to beg for is *not to be deaf to the call of the King!*

The temporal king[2] has as his greatest desire to conquer the world and he is looking for hard-working, generous, valiant soldiers to enlist and follow him. The victory will be that of the king, but he will share the victory with his faithful and hardworking followers.

Now the Eternal King is Jesus Christ, the Sovereign King of the Universe! Jesus launches the call to all who so desire to follow him. His pursuit, however, is not earthly gain, but something much more noble and eternal: the conquering and salvation of immortal souls! Jesus launches the invitation to all persons of good will.

This Ignatian contemplation of the call of the earthly king so as to hear the call of the Eternal King is a clarion and urgent *call to the apostolate.* This means that Jesus is calling all of us to work with him in the vineyard to gather

---

[2]   St. Ignatius uses this meditation as a springboard to follow Christ the King in a much more noble pursuit!

124

in a rich harvest. He is calling us to enter the boat and drop the nets so as to make a huge catch. The King calls us to be *fishers of men* (Lk 5:1–11).

Baptism and Confirmation: The Call to Extend the Kingdom

If you have been baptized and confirmed, then you are called to extend the kingdom of God, to spread the faith as well as defend the faith! In concrete, this is what it means to be called to the apostolate. As we follow from step to step in our professional and vocational plan of life, let us ask ourselves these simple but penetrating questions: *What am I doing to extend the kingdom of Christ, the Eternal King? What am I doing to work with the Eternal King in the most noble enterprise of saving souls?* The saints have a fire burning within them to work with Christ the King to glorify the Father, but also to save souls! The motto of Saint John Bosco was nothing less than this, posted on his wall: *Give me souls and take all the rest away!* Therefore, if we really do love God, then we should love what God loves—the salvation of immortal souls! Let us add this goal to the composition of our plan of life!

Before offering several apostolic initiatives, the motivational principle of Venerable Archbishop Fulton J. Sheen must prevail: *First Come, Then Go!* In other words, to be a successful apostle, a successful fisher of men, we must first come to Christ, get to know him, love him, and cherish a deep and dynamic relationship with him before we can give

him to others. That is to say, a rich apostolic life must flow
from a deep contemplative life. If you like, first the Mary,
then the Martha!

What then are some apostolic initiatives that we might
undertake in our following of the call of Jesus Christ, the
Lord of lords and the King of kings?

- **Catechism**. If you have sufficient preparation, offer
  your services to the pastor of your parish to teach catechism to children preparing to receive Jesus in Holy
  Communion. Recall to mind the words of Jesus: "Let
  the children come to me" (Mt 19:14).
- **Confirmation**. Perhaps you feel more of a pull to work
  with the challenging teens in the confirmation program.
  Prepare yourself well and work hard to save our young
  people from the deluge of materialism, hedonism, and
  confusion that inundates them. This is a most noble
  enterprise and very pleasing to the Lord Jesus.
- **Care for the Sick**. Go out of your way to visit the sick
  and offer them comfort and consolation. Jesus promises you a heavenly reward for this act of charity: "As
  you did it to one of the least of these my brethren, you
  did it to me" (Mt 25:40).
- **Bring Communion to the Sick, the Shut-Ins, Those
  in Hospitals or Nursing Homes**. Like the Blessed Virgin Mary who went to bring Jesus to her cousin Saint
  Elizabeth! In imitation of Mary, you can bring Jesus to
  those who cannot come to church or attend Holy Mass
  by bringing the Eucharistic Lord Jesus to them. What

a sublime apostolate! What a sublime gift you bring to them!

- **Liturgical Ministry and Apostolate**. Of course, the most sublime prayer that exists is the Holy Sacrifice of the Mass. The roles are various, but all are important, especially if we have purity of intention and do all for the honor and glory of God! Perhaps you feel called to offer your willing presence by engaging in some role at Mass, perhaps in the ministry of the Eucharist as an extraordinary minister of Holy Communion.

- **Lector**. Proclaim the Word of God by reading one of the Sunday Readings. Practice, prepare, and then cast out into the deep of God's Word, which is our light and our lamp!

- **Cantor**. If you have a good voice, offer to cantor at Mass or join one of the choirs. However, whatever the quality of your voice, it is the one God gave you, and it pleases him when you lift it in song at the Mass! Saint Augustine states that *he who sings prays twice* and *he who loves sings!* Sacred song can truly lift our minds and hearts to Almighty God!

- **Usher**. Offer your service to seat those who come to Sunday Mass, and be sure to do it with a smile! Ushers may also help with the Sunday collection, so necessary for the support of the parish!

- **Welcome!** There is a ministry that is dedicated to receiving people at the door and giving them a warm welcome. Although a humble service, it is very important, especially for newcomers to the parish, or visitors, or even someone who comes but is somewhat suspicious about the Catholic faith. Who knows, your warm greeting might win them over once and for all!

- **Altar Service.** The person who is at the side of the priest during the Mass—the altar boy—has an important role too. When altar boys are not available at weekday Mass, men in the parish often provide this important service for the priest. What a beautiful witness to the young people. All service is important in building up the Body of Christ and forming a harmonious symphony before God our Father.

- **Family Apostolate.** Changing gears slightly, why not become engaged in what we call *family apostolate.* By this we mean both husband and wife, father and mother, should make a constant and concerted effort to transmit the faith to their children, and to help their children participate actively, attentively, and fully in the Mass! Indeed, the parents are the first and primary educators in the family. God holds the parents responsible for the salvation of the immortal souls of their children!

As such we conclude with another block in our construction of an authentic plan of life—the apostolic life or the call to the apostolate. Jesus the Eternal King is calling you to labor with him for the salvation of immortal souls. Are you willing to accept the call and not be deaf to the call of the King?

17

EMBRACING A PENITENTIAL LIFESTYLE

JESUS said very clearly, "Unless you repent you will all likewise perish" (Lk 13:3). Also: "If any man would come after me, let him deny himself and take up his cross and follow me" (Mt 16:24). And of course, Jesus lived what he preached. He started off his public life with his baptism in the Jordan River, and immediately following his baptism, the Holy Spirit compelled him to go into the desert. While there for forty days and forty nights, Jesus prayed and fasted—went without eating or drinking. This is the foundational pillar of our Holy Season of Lent—forty days and forty nights of dedication to prayer and penance.

One of the primary purposes of our work in composing a plan of life is to help us pursue a life of holiness and once again to *order the disordered* in our lives. All of us are called to become saints; all of us are called to heavenly glory. Jesus asserted this unequivocally: "Be perfect, as your heavenly Father is perfect" (Mt 5:48). It is sufficient to read the life of one saint to be awed by their deep prayer life, as well as their dedication to penance and work. Saint Padre Pio, Saint John Vianney the Cure of Ars, Saint Faustina, Saint Francis of Assisi, Saint Ignatius of Loyola, and even the little children of Fatima—Saint Jacinta and Saint Francisco Marto—all practiced heroic penance.

They were motivated to imitate Jesus, as well as to work or collaborate with Jesus in the most noble enterprise of saving immortal souls. Indeed, if we truly love Jesus, we should love what he loves—the salvation of immortal souls. Jesus told Saint Faustina, "My daughter, I want to instruct you on how you are to rescue souls through sacrifice and prayer. You will save more souls through prayer and suffering than will a missionary through his teachings and sermons alone" (Diary of St. Faustina, 1767).[3]

Many Catholics have forgotten or maybe never learned that Friday is a day in which we are all called to carry out some form of penance in remembrance of all that Jesus willingly and lovingly suffered for us! Furthermore, recall once again the serious words of Jesus: "Unless you repent you will all likewise perish" (Lk 13:3).

Therefore, motivated by Jesus and all he endured for our sake, and by the lives of the saints, their prayers for us, their desire for our purification, as well as the salvation of immortal souls, we will dedicate this chapter in our work on the professional and vocational plan of life to carrying out some form of penance in our lives. May Our Lady of Fatima, the angels, and the saints intercede for us in this most noble and necessary initiative! This chapter will be straightforward in the sense that we will simply list various

---

[3]   Used with permission of the Marian Fathers of the Immaculate Conception of the B.V.M.

forms of penance you can undertake. Choose and pick, then implement them in your life. Friday is a day of obligatory penance, but that does not mean we cannot do penance on the other days of the week! These small sacrifices offered with love can be very pleasing to God and a source of our purification, as well as the salvation of many immortal souls!

- **The Palate—Our Taste for Food!** Give up at the table something you like to eat; it might be dessert. Instead of drinking a beverage, you might choose to drink water. Skip a meal during the day. At meal time, eat less! Maybe a third less than you normally eat! Condiments! Deprive yourself of condiments on your food: salt, pepper, mayo, mustard, salad dressing, cream and sugar, etc. Bread and water fast. With the consultation of a good spiritual director, perhaps you can assume the practice of this stricter fast one day a week.

- **Television.** Deprive yourself of some TV program you really like that you know is not necessary for the salvation of your soul, or possibly even detrimental to your salvation!

- **Electronic Devices.** Maybe you are too attached to your mobile phone, tablet, iPad, or laptop. A good act of penance might be to limit their use, at least on a certain day or days of the week.

- **Fasting of the Tongue.** This is always a great one! Try to avoid gossip, backbiting, lying, detraction—using the tongue as a means of destroying others; even if what you say is true, you have no right to say it. In other words, all the sins that we can so easily commit by the abuse of our tongue in speech.

- **Fasting of the Eyes**. There is a saying: *The eyes are the mirror of the soul.* Jesus leaves us this powerful verse from the Beatitudes: "Blessed are the pure in heart, for they shall see God" (Mt 5:8). Jesus went on to say, "The eye is the lamp of the body. So, if your eye is sound, your whole body will be full of light; but if your eye is not sound, your whole body will be full of darkness" (Mt 6:22–23). Therefore, try to make a concerted effort during the course of the day to look only at things that are pleasing to God—the true, the noble, and the beautiful!

- **Rise Earlier for Prayer**. Maybe it is such that your prayer life could be improved. How about getting up a few minutes earlier—maybe fifteen to twenty minutes—and give those first few minutes of the day to God in prayer, or add them to your holy hour if you already have that early morning practice! Be like Abel who gave God his best; he gave God his first fruits!

- **Kneel in Prayer**. Maybe you tend to seek comfort and ease in your life. Why not spend some of your prayer time on your knees? Remember what the athletes say: *No pain, no gain!* Be sure to offer this minor discomfort for the conversion and salvation of sinners! Our Lady of Fatima said that many souls are lost because not enough people pray for them and offer sacrifices for them. Jesus also told Faustina that souls are only saved by prayer and sacrifice. Little sacrifices, done with great love, have immense value before Almighty God!

- **Punctuality**. It might be that you are a person who is always running late, who is never on time. Due to this lack of consideration, you make people wait for you and waste their time. A really good penance could be to make a concerted effort to be punctual for your appointments, maybe even a few minutes early! It might be a penance for you, but it is an act of great charity and kindness to the persons who would otherwise be waiting for you. Jesus says, "He who is faithful in a very little is faithful also in much" (Lk 16:10).

- **Do Not Complain; Be Thankful!** Many suffer from that modern malady called *complainitus!* In other words, they find something wrong with everybody, every place, and every circumstance. Consequently, they are constantly complaining. Maybe, at least at times, you fit into that category of persons? Why not, as an act of penance, strive to avoid negativism and learn instead to thank others and thank God! If it is true that we can always find something to complain about, it is even more true that we can always find something to thank God for! Indeed, God loves a joyful and grateful heart! May this biblical passage be the inspiration for your life: "Give thanks to the LORD, for he is good; for his steadfast love endures for ever!" (Ps 107:1).

- **The Greatest Penance: Give Up Sin!** Of course, need-
  less to say, one of the greatest penances we can strive to
  carry out is to eliminate from our lives sin—that which
  most displeases God and most wounded Jesus on the
  cross! Examine your conscience and see what is your
  major moral failing—your most common sin[4]—and
  make war on yourself, with the help of God's grace, to
  conquer this sin! This is the true freedom of the sons
  and daughters of God!

In conclusion, to follow Jesus fully and completely, we
must also follow him on the way of the cross. We must
learn the art of renouncing our desires, our selfishness, our
self-will, and unite ourselves completely to our Lord who
carried the cross weighted down with all of the sins of the
world.

Therefore, read through the concrete acts of penance
mentioned above and, with the help of your spiritual director, decide upon a few that you will be able to incorporate
into your walk with the Lord. Remember in carrying out
penance the reason for it: our love for Jesus and our desire
to imitate him, as well as our desire to work with him for
the salvation of souls. May God bless you in this most noble
pursuit!

---

[4]   The publisher of this little book has an excellent manual designed to
       help you root out those sins to which you are most prone. It is called
       Manual for Conquering Deadly Sin.

18

AUGMENTING OUR SACRAMENTAL LIFE

O F course, we would be remiss if we did not visit and examine our personal sacramental life. As Catholics, the means by which we are sanctified most efficaciously are the sacraments present in the Church, which is the Mystical Body of Christ. There are three sacraments we can receive only once: Baptism, Confirmation, and Holy Orders. However, there are two sacraments we should form the habit of receiving frequently, faithfully, and fervently; these are the sacrament of God's mercy, confession, and the greatest of all the sacraments, the Holy Eucharist—the Body, Blood, Soul, and Divinity of Our Lord Jesus Christ!

If we are parents and our children have already made their First Communion and confession, then it is our moral obligation as parents to provide for our children's frequent access and availability to receive these powerhouses of grace for their sanctification and salvation. Indeed, Sunday Mass is a holy obligation; to fail to attend and bring your children is to sin gravely *twice*!

A Plan of Life for Our Sacramental Life

Monthly Confession. Make it a habit for you personally to have recourse to the sacrament of confession at least once a month, and more often if you fall into mortal sin.

Confession for Children. Bring your children at least once a month to the sacrament of confession. Remember the words of Jesus: "Let the children come to me" (Mt 19:14).

Sacrament of Devotion. Even when you don't have mortal sins to confess, you can confess your venial sins! The sacrament of confession or Reconciliation serves to augment sanctifying grace. Its primary effect is that of healing. In other words, it is medicine for the soul. However, it is not only *healing* medicine but *preventative* medicine as well!

Apostle of Confession. "Taste and see that the LORD is good!" (Ps 34:8). Confession fills our heart with a heavenly peace and sweetness. Why not become an apostle of the sacrament of confession and try to bring as many people as possible to this source of grace that we have? Bring back the wandering sheep; bring back the prodigal sons and daughters to the loving embrace of God the Father!

Pray for and Encourage Priests. Another part of your plan of life with respect to the sacramental life might be to simply pray for more priests, and priests who will be more available to hear confessions so as to reconcile sinners to God! May the great Saint John Bosco, Saint John Vianney, and Saint Alphonsus help us!

Mass and Holy Communion. Stop for a while and examine your relationship to our Eucharistic Lord. How can you fall deeper in love with the Lord of lords, the King of kings in the most Holy Sacrament of the Altar? One suggestion is this: every time you receive Jesus in Holy Communion, *beg our Blessed Mother* for the grace to love Jesus more and more with the purity and love of her own Immaculate Heart! This is a prayer she loves to answer!

How About Daily Mass and Communion? This topic should be repeated time and time again: love for the Mass, for the Eucharist, and for Holy Communion! In the Our Father, we pray, *Give us this day our Daily Bread.* This can obviously mean *daily Holy Communion.* The Psalmist invites us with these words, "As a deer longs for flowing streams, so longs my soul for you, O God" (Ps 42:1). May we long and yearn to receive Jesus in daily Holy Communion!

How About a Visit or Two During the Week? This also could be part of your plan of life—making a Eucharistic visit at least once during the week, if not more. The reason? To enkindle in your heart a fiery love for the Sacred Heart of Jesus truly present in the Eucharist!

Spiritual Communion. It is not always possible for all of us to attend Mass and receive Holy Communion on a daily basis. But none of us can exempt ourselves from at least making what is called a *spiritual communion.* The great Doctor of the Church Saint Alphonsus Liguori insists on this practice so as to fan the flame of our love for the Eucharistic Lord. Actually, making a spiritual communion has no time constraints or limits. You can make a spiritual communion in any time, in any place, using any words you like, and as often as you like. In your plan of life, reflect on a good time of the day to make at least one daily spiritual communion. If you need a formula to start: *Jesus, since I cannot receive you sacramentally, come spiritually into my heart. As if you were already come, I embrace you and unite myself entirely to you. Jesus, I love you. Jesus, I trust in you. Jesus, never let me be separated from you!*

Anniversaries of Sacramental Days. As followers of Our Lord and Savior Jesus Christ, we are called to live in joy and to rejoice and celebrate in a very special way our anniversary days. To fan the flames of your love for the Church and for the sacramental life, why not celebrate your special "family feast days", not only birthdays, but also anniversary dates of the days that you first received the sacraments? By doing this, you can pray that the grace first received in these sacraments will be renewed and that you will make a firmer commitment to live out the responsibilities that come with these sacraments. The following are examples of this concept:

- **Baptism Date**. Buy a cake and celebrate the day that you (or your children and loved ones) became a son or daughter of God, a living temple of the Blessed Trinity!
- **Confirmation Date**. Buy a pizza and rejoice for the outpouring of the Holy Spirit that was received on that day. Pray again earnestly: *Come, Holy Spirit, come through the Heart of Mary.*

- **First Communion Date**. Attend Mass with your family and make a fervent reception of Holy Communion on the day of the anniversary of your First Holy Communion. Give abundant thanks for this greatest gift of *Jesus Himself*, the *Bread of Life*, in Mass and Holy Communion. Beg pardon for your lack of appreciation. Recommit yourself to faith, love, and devotion in Mass and Holy Communion. Then, after spending time in thanksgiving after Mass, go out to a restaurant to celebrate!

- **Wedding Anniversary**. Every year married couples should humbly thank God for another year in the married state and vocation. Also, pray for future growth and love in your marriage, and faithfulness until death do you part! It is a beautiful custom to have a Mass offered in thanksgiving for another year of married life, thanksgiving for your children, and thanksgiving for the wonderful gift of faith. In your plan of life, renew your love for God, love for each other, and love for the children that God has given to you on the anniversary of your wedding day!

In conclusion, this chapter may be a unique but very powerful means of growing in your spiritual life by recovering an energetic commitment to your life in the Church through a renewed sacramental life. As Catholics, we should never downplay or underestimate the importance, the necessity, and the power of the sacraments in our spiritual life! Let us never take for granted these powerful gifts that Jesus has given to us. Let us turn to Mary, the Mother of the Church, the Mother of Grace, and the Mother of our Eucharistic Lord to help us set out a plan of life to appreciate and receive the sacraments with even greater love and fervor!

19

OUR LIFE WITH THE
BLESSED MOTHER

AT the moment of Mary's *yes* to become the Mother of the Messiah, by the power of the Holy Spirit, the Second Person of the Blessed Trinity became incarnate in her womb. The Angel told Mary, "You are to call him Jesus." For nine months, Mary protected the life of the baby Jesus growing within her womb, as his Sacred Heart beat beneath her Immaculate Heart. Just as she protected Jesus in her womb, Our Blessed Mother wants to protect us within her Immaculate Heart. For this reason, we want to consecrate ourselves totally to Jesus through Mary. Below are some of the ways we can stay within the Immaculate Heart of Mary until she brings us safely home to heaven.

Consecrating Yourself to Mary. Upon waking up every morning, your first action should be that of prayer, and what prayer? The Morning Offering should your first prayer upon waking, as pointed out in a previous chapter. Why not let your second prayer be one of entrusting and giving yourself totally to Jesus through the Immaculate Heart of Mary with this classic prayer of consecration:

O Mary, my Queen and my Mother, I give myself entirely to you, and to show my devotion to you, I consecrate to you my

141

eyes, my ears, my mouth, my heart, in other words, my whole being without reserve. Whereas I am your own dear Mother, keep me and guard me as your property and possession. Amen.

Also, do not forget to kiss and wear your Garment of Grace, the Scapular of Our Lady of Mount Carmel!

***Mariam Cogita, Mariam Invoca*—Think of Mary, Invoke Mary.** This is the classic maxim of the Oblates of the Virgin Mary. What better way to think of Mary and call on Mary than to pray a Hail Mary at the beginning of each hour of the day—it only takes ten seconds! Twelve seconds if you add a petition: *Mother, help me be patient today! Mother, pray for my son/daughter! Mother, pray for* _____ *who is having surgery today!* If you get busy and forget at the top of the hour, pray the Hail Mary as soon as you remember. Over time, this simple but powerful hourly prayer will become habitual, and you will be living constantly under the protection of Mary's mantel and pulling others under her mantle with your petitions!

The Angelus Prayer. This has been suggested before in our plan of life. The Angelus Prayer encompasses the sublime mystery of God's plan for our salvation in the Incarnation and the Paschal Mystery of the passion, death, and resurrection of Jesus Christ, Our Lord and Savior. By praying this prayer at 9 a.m. to sanctify the morning, 12 noon to sanctify the afternoon, and 6 p.m. to sanctify the evening, we give glory to God and honor to Mary, who is the daughter of the Father, mother of the Son, and mystical spouse of the Holy Spirit! As we pray this prayer daily, may we be moved to add our own prayer, recalling the proverb: *like Mother, like daughter/son:*

> "Behold the servant of the Lord, be it done *unto me* according to your word! May the Word, Jesus, be made flesh *in me* – in spirit and in Holy Communion! May he dwell among us because *I bring him to others!* And through Mary's prayers, may I be made worthy of the promises of Christ and brought to the glory of his resurrection!"

The Angelus Prayer:

The Angel of the Lord declared to Mary,
And she conceived of the Holy Spirit.

Pray the Hail Mary.

Behold the handmaid of the Lord,
Be it done unto me according to Thy word.

Pray the Hail Mary.

And the Word was made Flesh,
And dwelt among us.

Pray the Hail Mary.

Pray for us, O Holy Mother of God,
That we may be made worthy of the promises of Christ.

Let us pray: Pour forth, we beseech Thee, O Lord, Thy grace into our hearts; that we, to whom the Incarnation of Christ, Thy Son, was made known by the message of an angel, may by His Passion and Cross be brought to the glory of His Resurrection, through the same Christ Our Lord. Amen.

Another Exhortation to Pray the Rosary Daily! To love Mary is to obey what she requests of us. Love is shown in actions! In the approved apparitions of Our Lady at Lourdes and at Fatima, she asked the children, as well as us who are also her children, to pray the Rosary every day—for the conversion of sinners, in reparation for our sins and the sins of others, and for world peace! At work or at home, why not take a *fifteen-minute break* each day and pray the Rosary! If you can, take a *fifteen-minute walk* and pray the Rosary; get some fresh air and sunshine for your body and your soul! Better yet, pray the Rosary as a family in the evening! Call to mind the words of the renowned Rosary priest Venerable Father Patrick Peyton: *The family that prays together, stays together.* And: *A world at prayer is a world at peace.*

Our Lady of the Way. Finally, Saint Ignatius of Loyola had a special devotion to Mary under the title of *Madonna della Strada* ("Our Lady of the Way"). An image of the Blessed Virgin Mary under this name is enshrined in the church of the Gesù in Rome, mother church of the Society of Jesus, the Jesuits, the religious order founded by Saint Ignatius. This image of Mary reminds us that wherever we go in life, we want to invite Mary to be with us—to walk with us, talk with us, listen to us, console us, love us, protect us—until we arrive safely at our heavenly reward, eternal life in the glory of the Father, Son, and Holy Spirit, with our Blessed Mother Mary, Saint Joseph, and all the angels and saints, including loved ones already there, who even now are eagerly praying for us and awaiting our arrival!

CONCLUSION

THE WONDERFUL EFFECTS
OF A PLAN OF LIFE

THE positive effects of a well-ordered, methodical, systematic, practical, and concrete plan of life are very
many and worthy of praise. However, it must be empha-
sized that the plan of life you have written out and your
spiritual director has approved is not simply some aca-
demic, theoretical, *pie in the sky* exercise that goes up in
smoke after being composed. On the contrary, the primary
purpose of the plan of life is to implement it in your life,
make it a part of your life, and allow it to influence the way
you think, decide, act, and live out the short life that God
has given to you so that you may arrive at your eternal destiny, heaven!

Therefore, as a last note of encouragement, we would
like to highlight the many wonderful effects of the plan of
life you have decided to reflect upon, organize, compose,
and write out, with the help of your spiritual director, who
represents the Lord himself.

- **Peace of Heart, Mind, Soul**. The great Saint Augustine,
  who lived an unruly, lustful, and sinful life up into his
  early thirties, understood in his own flesh and bones

the reality of disorder. After his conversion, he went on to become one of the greatest intellectuals and writers in the Catholic Church, as well as the world at large. Among many things, he said this: *peace is the tranquility of order.* Therefore, your plan of life will produce peace in the depths of your heart, mind, and soul. All of us ardently yearn for peace. This peace that we long for comes from God and is one of the fruits of the Holy Spirit. Jesus visited the Apostles on Easter day with the greeting: *Shalom,* meaning, *Peace be with you!* May your plan of life fill you with a constant and all-abiding peace!

- **Purpose in Life**. Saint Ignatius of Loyola, in his reflection "Principle and Foundation" (*Spiritual Exercises,* no. 23) states the purpose of our existence in these words: "Man is created to praise, reverence, and serve God our Lord, and by this means save his soul." Your plan of life will be of great utility in helping you, better yet, in motivating you to pursue seriously, in an orderly and methodical fashion, the salvation of your immortal soul for all eternity!

- **Goal and Purpose**. The plan of life that you have written out—chronological or professional and vocational (or both)—will help you enormously in having short-term, as well as long-term, goals. Many live like the proverbial *chicken running around with its head cut off!* The plan of life constantly points us to that destination for which God made us. If you like a modern analogy, our plan of life serves as a *spiritual GPS*. It is a clear and certain spiritual road map that zooms us along the highway to heaven.

- **Avoid Wasting Time.** As mentioned during the course of this work, *time is of the essence*. Our life on earth is ephemeral—meaning it is passing and very short. Even if we were to live one hundred years and beyond, our life in comparison with eternity is nothing! For that reason, the great Saint Augustine says that our life in comparison with eternity is a mere blink of the eye. Saint James uses another graphic but powerful image: our life is like a mere puff of smoke blown by the wind and gone!

- **Conquer Laziness.** A lazy person flounders in no man's land and gets nowhere with his life. Whereas the person who is sincerely trying to live out their plan of life as their moral compass and guide will find it much easier to avoid giving in to laziness and wasting the time that God has so generously given to them. An authentic plan of life vitalizes and fortifies the will with good proposals and conquers the innate laziness that we have inherited from our first parents, Adam and Eve, and possibly a poor family upbringing.

- **Our Actions Are Done Well the First Time.** There is a Spanish proverb: *El perezoso trabaja doble*—translation: the person who is lazy ends up by working double! Why is this? For the simple reason that without planning and method—without a plan of life—actions are done poorly and often must be done over, thus wasting valuable time!

- **Do Not Waste Energy**. It is also worthy of note that the person who valiantly undertakes to write out and live a plan of life wastes neither time nor energy. We all have experienced how failing at a project as a result of disorder knocks the wind out of our sails. On the contrary, when a project is well done in good time, we are energized and have energy to exert efficaciously for other enterprises!

- **Interior Joy in Accomplishment**. All of us have experienced the joy of having completed some project, whether big or seemingly small and unimportant. Examples: finishing praying a Rosary, cleaning the bathroom or cleaning the house, finishing homework, cutting the grass, passing an exam after studying hard, shoveling snow to clear the sidewalk, graduating from school whether Elementary, High School, or College— all of these goals, once reached, produce in our heart a great sense of joy because we have accomplished our objective. Likewise, our plan of life helps us to carry out our long- and short-term spiritual goals, and with these accomplishments, we experience joy of heart!

- **Motivation and Momentum to Accomplish More**. Indeed, it is very true that when we are on a roll, when we have momentum, when we have wind in our sails and we are accomplishing much, this is motivation to accomplish even more. When we can see a successful task, job, or enterprise well done before our eyes, it fills us with the desire to do even more and do our work even better.

- **Order the Disordered**. One of the key, so to speak, *Antiphons* of our work has been the Ignatian theme found in the *Spiritual Exercises* "Order the Disordered." Therefore, if your plan of life is well-planned, well-written, implemented, and lived out generously, then beyond the shadow of a doubt, your life will start to take on greater order. The mosaic of your life will be seen with greater clarity and beauty. The broken jigsaw puzzle of a disjointed existence will be re-assembled in a superb symmetry. The misty and cloudy pathway of your life will shine with the sunlight of God's all-encompassing presence! This is the glorious and fulfilling call of the saints, and we are all called to be saints!

- **Apostolic Fruitfulness**. It also must be said that this plan of life is really a gift that you want to give to God. Like the first fruits of Abel, rather than the leftovers of Cain, this plan of life can be considered your offering, the first fruits of your life to the Creator of all. We have demonstrated how an ordered, contemplative prayer life leads to an ordered apostolic life—*First Come, Then Go*—as so succinctly expressed by Venerable Archbishop Fulton J. Sheen. Reflected in the lives of the saints is a deep prayer life leading to great order, energy, and purpose in all of their projects, plans, and actions. It is incredible, almost overwhelming, to see how much the saints accomplished and sometimes with very little resources, often very little time, and at times confronted with many obstacles from within and from without. Why and how? For this reason. The Holy Spirit is a God of order; the Holy Spirit is a God of energy and strength; the Holy Spirit is a God of wisdom and intelligence; and the Holy Spirit is our Helper! "Our help is in the name of the LORD, who made heaven and earth" (Ps 124:8). Even if it were such that all of the saints did not have an exterior written plan of life, they at least had some plan of life interiorized! Read the lives of the saints: Saint Mother Teresa, Saint Teresa of Avila, Saint Thomas Aquinas, Saint Alphonsus Liguori, Pope St. John Paul II, Saint Maximillian Kolbe, and many others. How close they were to God and how much good they did for others and for the salvation of souls! Lest we be daunted by these giants in the spiritual life, let us not forget our youngest saints, Saint Jacinta and Saint Francisco Marto! Certainly, with the witness and prayers of the saints, the help of an able spiritual director, and led by the Holy Spirit in writing out and living a generous plan of life, we can become the saints God intended us to be from all eternity! May our Blessed Mother Mary, who suffered in her Immaculate Heart all that Jesus suffered in his body for our salvation, sustain us in this most noble adventure!

• **Save Souls!** Indeed, if we do truly love God, then we should love what God loves: the salvation of immortal souls! For the sake of the wandering sheep, the prodigal sons and daughters of the world who are heading toward the precipice of hell, or even now standing at the very edge of that precipice, let us determine right here and now to live a well-ordered, well-thought-out plan of life that can help us work with the Lord of lords and the King of kings in pursuit of the salvation of immortal souls. Never forget what Saint Thomas Aquinas teaches: one soul is worth more than the whole created universe! Your plan of life, well-lived, working side-by-side with Our Lord Jesus, can serve for the salvation of many forlorn and confused souls who are slaves of sin and heading for the precipice.

In conclusion, our hope, our desire, and our fervent prayers are for all of you most generous souls who, with courage and great trust in God, have read prayerfully our humble work and are choosing to embark on this new venture of the plan of life! We pray that you will find a spiritual director to guide you. We hope and pray that you will take time in prayerful silence to compose this wonderful and life-changing proposal, your own personal plan of life!

We believe most firmly that if you seriously undertake this most noble spiritual project and honestly strive to live it out, your life will be radically transformed. The Holy Spirit, through the intercession of the Blessed Virgin Mary, the Mother of God, the Mother of the Church, and our own heavenly mother, will fill you with heavenly lights in your intellect, a burning fire in your heart, peace that passes all understanding, most abundant personal, family, and apostolic fruits, and a rich and abundant harvest of salvation for immortal souls who will enter joyfully into the kingdom of God. May Our Lady bless you, look down upon you tenderly, and embrace you dearly in her Immaculate Heart.

DAILY AND WEEKLY PLAN OF LIFE FOR YOUTH

A LL of us are called to grow in holiness, calling to mind the words of Jesus: "Be perfect, as your heavenly Father is perfect" (Mt 5:48). At the same time, we all have different stages in our spiritual growth. A seed is planted, sprouts, and grows gradually into full stature—into a tree, a plant, a flower, etc. The seed planted in Baptism must be cultivated lest it wither and die.

Our young people are called to holiness. Saint Dominic Savio, Saint Maria Goretti, and Saints Jacinta and Francisco Marto are all examples of how young people, teens, and even children can arrive at holiness, even in a short time.

We are all born with original sin and experience its negative effects. Among the most notable are the capital sins—gluttony, greed, lust, laziness, anger, envy, and pride. These are already manifest in children and teens. If not restrained, these capital sins transform into actual sins, and eventually slavery.

Therefore, as a positive and powerful step in the right direction, parents must write out and strive to live their own plan of life. However, parents should also present to their children, especially the teens, as presented in this chapter, a concrete plan of life that is simple, practical, and feasible—one they are capable of carrying out.

Time and time again you have been reading and reflecting on the words of Saint Ignatius of Loyola: *Order the disordered!* This must be applied to the young, to the teens, to the future adults.

One of the great benefits of a plan of life is that of forming good habits. A good habit, we call a *virtue;* a bad habit, we call a *vice.* It is incumbent upon parents to plant and cultivate solid, deeply rooted virtues in the lives of their children and teens. We all know from sad experience how difficult it is to overcome deeply entrenched, deeply rooted bad habits that we started while young. Drinking to excess, smoking, problems with porn, over-eating, vulgar language and jokes, shopping till we drop—all are a few of the many vices that can indeed dominate us, even enslave us. Now is the time to plant good habits deeply in the minds, hearts, and lives our children and teens.

Therefore, this appendix will concentrate on helping the teens, with the help of their parents, to choose and hammer out a plan of life. It is much easier to bend a tree when it is young or a sapling than when it is fully grown. So it is with the human person! Easier to form habits when we are young, tender, and docile, than when the years are upon us!

The nature of this plan of life embodies two important parts: 1) the five m's daily; 2) fifteen minutes with Jesus and Mary daily.

The First Part of the Teen Plan of Life: The Five M's!

We will present a rather simple plan of life for the teens utilizing alliteration: *The Five M's!*

- **Morning Prayer.** The youth, the teens, must start off their day with prayer. Let their first words be an Act of Consecration of themselves to Jesus through the Blessed Virgin Mary. Let the teens wear their scapular—the outward sign of consecration to Mary—and kiss it in conjunction with their Morning Offering. This is a great way to start off the day—giving one's total self to Jesus through the Immaculate Heart of Mary. Here is a short prayer that Mary loves to hear and answer: *O Mary, my Queen and my Mother, I give myself entirely to you, and to show my devotion to you, I consecrate to you my eyes, my ears, my mouth, my heart, in other words, my whole being without reserve. Whereas I am your own dear Mother, keep me and guard me this day. Amen.*
- **Meal Blessing.** This prayer habit depends mostly upon mom and dad and their prayer habits. Nevertheless, teens and children should not start to eat without first offering a short prayer of gratitude to God for his goodness in providing for their daily nourishment, their daily bread. *Give us this day our daily bread.*
- **Meditation on the Bible: The Word of God.** May all good Catholic parents purchase a good Catholic Bible for their teens and have it blessed by a priest. The Bible,

the Word of God, is the daily love letter of God to his children! As such, parents should strongly encourage their teens to read the Bible frequently, better yet, daily! Invite your teens to start with five to ten minutes a day. If they want to go beyond those few minutes and extend to fifteen minutes, or even to a half hour, praise the Lord! The following might be a simple method for the teens to derive abundant fruit from reading and meditating upon the Bible—God's Holy Word. Start with the Gospels—Matthew, Mark, Luke, and John. Take a chapter every day and follow this method: 1) Say a prayer before reading (e.g., the Our Father or Hail Mary); 2) Read and listen, *Speak, O Lord, for your servant is listening* (1 Sm 2:10); 3) Think about what the message is, what God is saying to you; 4) Talk to God from your heart about what he is saying to you and how you might respond to him; 5) Apply! Move from your prayer to your feet! Try to put into practice God's message to you!

- **Mass and Holy Communion.** Parents must teach their teens very clearly, cogently, and convincingly that the greatest prayer in the whole universe is that of the Holy Sacrifice of the Mass. Sunday is the Lord's Day and it is the most important day of the week, for it is the day that as Catholics we go to Mass to give adoration and thanksgiving to God! The culminating moment in Holy Mass is the reception of Jesus in Holy Communion—his Body, Blood, Soul, and Divinity! Encourage your teens, whenever possible, to go to Mass an extra day of the week—highlighting its importance! Our salvation depends on the Mass and the Eucharist—the Bread of Life! The words of Jesus must be taken very seriously: "I am the bread of life; he who comes to me shall not hunger, and he who believes in me shall never thirst" (Jn 6:35).

- **Mary and the Rosary**. Inculcate in your teens a fervent, filial, and confident love for the Blessed Virgin Mary. This can be translated into the daily recitation of the most Holy Rosary. In 1917 Our Lady of Fatima appeared six times to three little shepherd children— Lucia de los Santos and Francisco and Jacinta Marto. At every appearance, Our Lady of Fatima insisted on the praying of the most Holy Rosary. Even though hard, demanding, and not an overly emotional prayer, if the teens take seriously their devotion to Mary by praying the most Holy Rosary, the Blessed Mother will attain very special graces for them now, and in the end, final perseverance in grace and eternal salvation!

We hope that parents will undertake the proposition to help their teens carry out the first part of this plan of life. The use of alliteration with *the Five M's* makes it easy to remember and not overly difficult to live out.

Remember the big *Five M's: morning prayer, meal blessing, meditation on the Bible, Mass and Holy Communion, Mary and the Rosary!* Here you have a winner for the challenges facing our teens! Now on to the second part of this plan of life for the teens, equally important and powerful!

The Second Part of the Teen Plan of Life: Fifteen Minutes With Jesus and Mary!

We will present a step-by-step guide to help the teens enter daily into conversation with their Best Friends—Jesus and Mary!

Jesus and Mary are your *Best Friends* always, in all places and in all times. You can talk to them and confide in them always! And Jesus and Mary are always ready and willing to listen to you and talk to you as friends do. At the Last Supper, Jesus said to the apostles (as well as to you and me): "I have called you friends" (Jn 15:15). His friendship has not changed in over two thousand years and it will never change. Jesus and Mary have a great longing, a great desire, in this precise moment to enter into a conversation of friendship with you.

Now place yourself in the presence of Jesus and Mary. Imagine that they are looking at you with great tenderness, kindness, and love. Lift your eyes, as well as your heart, to the images of Jesus and Mary. Now open up your heart and talk to Jesus and Mary. Tell them everything that is in your mind, everything that is in your heart, and what is going on in your life. They are the best of listeners!

As a means to help you, imagine now that Jesus and Mary, with their great love for you, ask you some very simple questions. And you respond to these questions in your own words. Your words can be simple, uncomplicated, humble, and sincere. Here we go with your loving conversation with Jesus and with his mother, and your Mother, the Blessed Virgin Mary.

- **Who Are You?** Why not start with the basics? Jesus asks you: *Who are you? What is your name? Where do you live? What family do you come from? How old are you now? When is your birthday? Where do you go to school? What grade are you in?* With these most simple and basic questions, you are opening up and talking to Jesus and Mary. They are listening very attentively to your words, even to the movements of your heart. You can speak to Jesus and Mary as long as you want. They are in no hurry; they have no time schedule. You are important to them!

- **What Is on Your Mind Now?** In all times and places, something is crossing our mind; our mind is never totally blank. Right now, why not express to Jesus and Mary the thoughts that are crossing or running through your mind. Then tell them: Do these thoughts bring you joy or sadness, peace or confusion? Talk to them sincerely about your "thought" world.

- **Are You Fearful?** We all go through moments of fear about many things. Perhaps over the past few days there has been something in your life that has caused you to enter into a state of fear. This is an excellent topic of conversation between you and Jesus and Mary. Often the apostles had fears; all people have fears in their lives. So do you and so do I. Bring these fears to the hearts of Jesus and Mary. What might be some of these fears? Fears can come in many shapes and forms, colors and shades. Never forget that both Jesus and Mary love you always and are always ready to listen to you and to help you. Here are a few that might be common to young people. Your future? Are you worried about your future? Talk to Jesus and Mary about that. A test or exam you have to take and pass? Talk to Jesus and Mary about your studies and ask for light, ask for help. Is there someone at school whom you do not like and who does not like you? This tension between you and this person may be causing you fears and uncertainties. Talk to Jesus about this person. Jesus had many friends, but he also had many enemies who actually put him to death.

- **Other Fears?** Family tensions and problems? Your fears might not be in school but in your home, in your own family. Maybe there is tension, turmoil, bitterness, and anger among some family members and this is a constant cause of fear and anxiety in your mind and heart. Open up your heart to Jesus and Mary and talk to them about these family tensions and fears. Talk to Jesus and Mary about your family members. Most likely there is especially one family member most in need of your prayers. Tell Jesus and Mary about this brother or sister, mom or dad. The hearts of Jesus and Mary are very attentive to your prayers.

- **Wounds of the Past, Wounds in the Present**. Because of the original sin of our first parents, Adam and Eve, we all live in a world that is deeply wounded. And that means that we too are wounded, and most likely we have wounded others. Most likely, even now, you carry wounds in your heart. Being abused, in many ways, leaves big, gaping wounds. Now is the time to bring these wounds to the Sacred Heart of Jesus that was pierced by the lance and the Immaculate Heart of Mary who suffered the wounds of Jesus in her heart as she stood beneath the cross. If we are physically beaten, sexually abused, emotionally hurt, socially rejected, neglected by parents, or even bullied in one form or another, all of these leave wounds that can be very deep.

- **Jesus the Wounded Healer**. Now Jesus is the *Wounded Healer*. In prayer, we can bring these many, and possibly big, wounds to Jesus. The Bible says: "With his stripes we are healed" (Is 53:5). Do not be afraid to open up and talk to Jesus about your wounds because *by his wounds we are healed*. Call to mind the many sick, suffering, and wounded people who came to Jesus while he walked the earth. Jesus was moved to compassion and he healed them, if they trusted in him. Imagine that you are one of those wounded and sick in the time of Jesus: the blind, the deaf, the mute, the leper, the paralytic! Like them, go to Jesus and ask for healing.

Go to the Immaculate Heart of Mary and ask her to heal you. Mary is known as *Refuge of sinners, Health of the sick, and Mother of mercy and consolation.* Turn to Mary as your loving Mother, open your wounded heart and talk to her.

- **Your Temptations.** Talk to Jesus and Mary about your temptations! Do not be ashamed in your conversation with Jesus and Mary to talk to them about your temptations. Everybody in the world is subject to temptations, and until the very end of our lives. The devil never goes on vacation! A temptation is not a sin until we give in to it. Bring to Jesus and Mary the many temptations you are experiencing. Here might be a few. Temptations to give in to discouragement; bring this to the Heart of Jesus. Temptations to give in to impurity; bring this to the Immaculate Heart of Mary. Temptations to laziness; talk to Jesus about this. Temptations to impatience; turn to Jesus who carried the cross patiently and beg for his help. Temptations to lie; turn for help to Jesus who said: "I am the way, and the truth, and the life" (Jn 14:6). Temptations to disobey; run to Jesus who was obedient even to death, and death on the cross! Bringing your temptations to Jesus and Mary are great ways to overcome the devil!

- **Even Your Sins!** Now this is a very important topic of conversation with Jesus and Mary: your sins! Jesus did not come for the perfect; He came to save sinners. The name *Jesus* means *God Saves!* The worst thing we can do is to fail to *trust* in Jesus and his love and mercy. Therefore, bring even your failures, your sins, to the most Merciful Hearts of Jesus and Mary. Tell Jesus that you love him and that you are sorry for these sins. Tell him that you want to change. Beg Jesus for the grace and strength to change. Then also tell Jesus about your desire to go to confession and begin again. The prophet Isaiah encourages us with these words spoken by the Lord: "Though your sins are like scarlet, they shall be as white as snow" (Is 1:18). Say the following words often to Jesus, words that give great consolation to the Sacred Heart of Jesus and Immaculate Heart of Mary: "Jesus, I trust in you!"

- **Your Plans, Your Goals, Your Dreams**. As young people, we should all have plans, goals, and even dreams. We should have long term goals, short term goals, and dreams that we want to accomplish. Jesus and Mary are very interested in these. Open up your heart and talk to Jesus and Mary about these. Talk to them about a college you might want to attend. Your profession in life? Tell Jesus and Mary what you might like to be once you come to the end of your high school and college years. Doctor, lawyer, teacher, engineer, architect, writer, athlete—all of these are noble aspirations and goals. Maybe you're thinking about the priesthood or religious life? Why not open up and talk to Jesus and Mary about your future goals and projects? They are very interested in your future and want to help you make the right choices in life. Open up and talk to them about your future!

- **Thanksgiving: An Attitude of Gratitude.** Jesus and Mary rejoice when we tell them these two words: *thank you*! Therefore, try to get into the habit of thanking Jesus and Mary for so many gifts that they have given to you. In sum, what do we have that we have not received from God? Nothing! Except our own sins that we have freely chosen. Stop now, look up to Jesus and Mary, and pour out your heart in gratitude!

- **Imitate the One Grateful Leper.** On one occasion, ten lepers came to Jesus and he healed the ten, but only one came back to give Jesus thanks! May you be that one grateful leper! Thank Jesus and Mary for your life; *Thank you, Jesus and Mary!* Give thanks for your health; *Lord Jesus, thanks!* Give thanks for your family; *Lord, I lift up my hands in thanks!* For freedom; *Jesus, once again, thanks!* For your Catholic faith; *Lord, from the depths of my heart, thank you!*

- **Become the Beggar Before Jesus.** Beggars would sometimes approach Jesus and he would often grant what they requested. Now it is your turn to become the beggar! Jesus said: "Ask, and it will be given you; seek, and you will find; knock, and the door will be opened to you" (Mt 7:7). Any need that is in your heart, open up and become a beggar before Jesus. He loves to help humble and trusting beggars.

- **Beg for Others**. Do not limit your prayers to yourself. Rather, go outside yourself and beg for the intentions of others, for the needs of others. Beg for a sick grandma; beg for world peace; beg for hungry children; beg for the sick and the dying in the world; beg for the homeless and the orphans. Beg also for the souls in purgatory. Beg for the conversion of poor sinners. Many graces descend into the world due to the prayers of the beggars!

- **Love Jesus and Mary**. The most important sentiment that can flow from our hearts is that of love. Jesus said the greatest commandment is to love God with all our heart, mind, soul, and strength. Never forget how much Jesus and Mary love you. However, in your own words, you should tell them how much you really do love them. Love is the bond of perfection. Saint John of the Cross says, "In the twilight of our life, we will be judged on love." In your own words, tell Jesus and Mary right now how much you love them. Beg them for the grace to love them more and more each day. Beg Jesus and Mary for the grace to love them now, tomorrow, and forever in heaven!

APPENDIX OF PRAYERS

Sign of the Cross

In the name of the Father, and of the Son, and of the Holy Spirit. Amen.

Our Father

Our Father, who art in heaven, hallowed be thy name; thy kingdom come, thy will be done, on earth as it is in heaven. Give us this day our daily bread and forgive us our trespasses, as we forgive those who trespass against us and lead us not into temptation, but deliver us from evil. Amen.

Hail Mary

Hail Mary, full of grace, the Lord is with thee. Blessed art thou among women and blessed is the fruit of thy womb, Jesus. Holy Mary, mother of God, pray for us sinners now and at the hour of our death. Amen.

Glory Be

Glory be to the Father, and to the Son, and to the Holy Spirit. As it was in the beginning, is now, and ever shall be, world without end. Amen.

Apostles' Creed

I believe in God, the Father almighty, creator of heaven and earth, and in Jesus Christ, his only Son, our Lord, who was conceived by the Holy Spirit, born of the Virgin Mary, suffered under Pontius Pilate, was crucified, died, and was buried. He descended into hell; the third day he rose again from the dead; he ascended into heaven and is seated at the right hand of the Father; from thence he shall come to judge the living and the dead. I believe in the Holy Spirit, the holy Catholic Church, the communion of saints, the forgiveness of sins, the resurrection of the body, and life everlasting. Amen.

The Rosary

Joyful Mysteries

- The Annunciation
- The Visitation
- The Birth of Jesus
- The Presentation
- The Finding of the Lost Child Jesus in the Temple

Luminous Mysteries

- The Baptism in the River Jordan
- The Miracle at Cana
- Proclamation of the Kingdom
- The Transfiguration
- The Institution of the Eucharist

Sorrowful Mysteries

- The Agony in the Garden
- The Scourging at the Pillar
- The Crowning with Thorns
- The Carrying of the Cross
- The Crucifixion

Glorious Mysteries

- The Resurrection
- The Ascension
- The Descent of the Holy Spirit
- The Assumption
- The Crowning of Mary as the Queen of Heaven

Hail Holy Queen

Hail, Holy Queen, Mother of mercy, our life, our sweetness, and our hope. To thee do we cry, poor banished children of Eve. To thee do we send up our sighs, mourning and weeping in this valley of tears. Turn then, most gracious advocate, thine eyes of mercy towards us and after this, our exile, show unto us the blessed fruit of thy womb, Jesus. O clement, O loving, O sweet Virgin Mary.

V. Pray for us, O holy Mother of God.

R. That we may be made worthy of the promises of Christ.

The Memorare

Remember, O most gracious Virgin Mary, that never was it known that anyone who fled to thy protection, implored thy help, or sought thy intercession was left unaided. Inspired with this confidence, we fly unto thee, O Virgin of virgins, our Mother. To thee we come, before thee we stand, sinful and sorrowful. O Mother of the Word Incarnate, despise not our petitions, but in thy mercy hear and answer us.

The Angelus

The angel of the Lord declared unto Mary.

R. And she conceived of the Holy Spirit. (Hail Mary . . .)

Behold the handmaid of the Lord.

R. Be it done unto me according to thy word. (Hail Mary . . .)

And the Word was made flesh.

R. And dwelt among us. (Hail Mary . . .)

Pray for us, O holy Mother of God.

R. That we may be made worthy of the promises of Christ.

Let us pray: Pour forth, we beseech thee, O Lord, thy grace into our hearts; that we, to whom the incarnation of Christ, thy Son, was made known by the message of an angel, may by his passion and cross, be brought to the glory of his resurrection, through the same Christ our Lord. Amen.

Grace Before Meals

Bless us, O Lord, and these thy gifts, which we are about to receive, from thy bounty, through Christ, our Lord. Amen.

Prayer to Our Guardian Angel

Angel of God, my guardian dear, to whom God's love commits me here, ever this day be at my side to light, to guard, to rule and guide. Amen.

Prayer to Saint Michael the Archangel

St. Michael the Archangel, defend us in battle; be our protection against the wickedness and snares of the devil. May God rebuke him, we humbly pray, and do thou, O prince of the heavenly host, by the power of God, thrust into hell Satan and all evil spirits who prowl about the world seeking the ruin of souls. Amen.

The Devotion of the Three Hail Marys

This devotion is one that is somewhat forgotten in the Church today, but it should not be. Great saints have made it their own including Saint Gertrude the Great to whom the Blessed Mother appeared, promising that, at the hour of death of those who were devoted to the practice, she would appear and bring those souls heavenly consolation. Saint Leonard of Port Maurice fostered the more particular practice of praying three Hail Marys morning and evening to avoid mortal sins, especially those of impurity. Upon waking, recite three Hail Marys, concluding with: "O My Mother, preserve me from mortal sin during this day." And in the evening before going to bed, recite the three Hail Marys, concluding with: "O My Mother, preserve me from mortal sin during this night."